THE
LAUNCH
BUTTON

THE
LAUNCH
BUTTON

Start Here to Fire Your Boss,
Pursue Your Passions Full-Time,
and Build the Life of Your Dreams

HUGH ZARETSKY

HOUNDSTOOTH
PRESS

THE LAUNCH BUTTON
Start Here to Fire Your Boss, Pursue Your Passions Full-Time, and Build the Life of Your Dreams

ISBN   978-1-5445-3480-0 *Hardcover*

       978-1-5445-3481-7 *Paperback*

       978-1-5445-3482-4 *Ebook*

Contents

Disclaimer

THE MATERIALS CONTAINED IN THIS BOOK HAVE BEEN prepared for informational purposes only. Prior results do not guarantee a similar outcome. This material does not constitute the offering of legal or financial advice. Reviewing this information is not a substitute for obtaining the advice of an attorney, CPA, financial planner, or life insurance expert. Hugh highly recommends you contact one before taking action or implementing these ideas.

INTRODUCTION

An Average Day

It Takes Courage to Start

Everything you have ever wanted in your life is just on the other side of fear. Are you willing to push through to grab it?

JUST IMAGINE A BEAUTIFUL TUESDAY MORNING IN NEW YORK City. The sun is shining. There is not a cloud in the sky, and the temperature is just about perfect. You are "high on life" as you have just moved into a luxury apartment with a pool on the roof! You no longer have to commute two hours each way to get to work. You have also recently been promoted and now have a corner office plus additional stock options in a publicly traded company. You are making more money than ever, all under the age of thirty.

You are seated in a glass-walled conference room with your team, going over their weekly updates. As you look out over the stylish office with bright splashes of colors, you feel content and satisfied. Suddenly, you see a few people outside the conference room run to the building's exterior windows and look up at the New York City skyline. You try to ignore them at first, but more people keep running over to the windows. You decide to stop the meeting and let everyone see what the fuss is about. When you get to the windows, you can't believe what you are seeing. There is a massive, smoking hole in the side of one of the Twin Towers.

Some members of your team stare out the windows in shock, as they had just commuted through the bottom of the towers less than thirty minutes earlier. You immediately feel yourself going into firefighter mode. As the leader, you have to keep everyone calm and safe and figure out a plan to keep the systems and IT network up and running. Just as you start giving directions to your team, you see a second plane fly past the window and then directly into the second tower. It explodes into a fireball. As you turn, a colleague collapses, and you are able to catch her before she hits the floor. You carry her over to her desk chair, where she begins to sob. The adrenaline starts pulsing through your body as you know the company's photographers will be running down to the Twin Towers to cover the scene. Your team has to help get those photos out to the world, which means you have to keep the IT systems and network working for as long as possible, so the news team can process and distribute pictures. You have to keep your team safe and start the emergency procedures to transfer all of the data to corporate headquarters in Seattle. You have to wake up the CTO and the entire IT team. All the while, you still do not know what is going on or if there will be another plane.

Fast-forward, and you have just gotten back to the office after taking the only digital camera up to the roof of the building to shoot photos of the holes in the towers. You sit there watching the picture desk editors process your photos and all of the photos coming in from the real photographers. Suddenly, one of them gasps out loud. Everyone turns to look at the picture she is working on. It is a photo of a group of people jumping from one of the towers. Their choice was to jump or burn to death.

You suddenly realize this could have been you except for the grace of God, spirit, the universe, or whatever you believe in. The only reason it isn't you is because the company you worked for signed a lease in a smaller building. Those people in the Twin Towers all had hopes and dreams that they will never fulfill. You realize that you have to change, because there has to be a better way and more to life than being stuck in an office with a choice to either jump or burn.

September 11, 2001, is the day that changed my life. I will not go into more details right now about the things I saw, the stupid things I did, or what I encountered that day. What I will tell you is it was the catalyst that forced me out of my cushy, corporate comfort zone and jump-started the journey that encouraged me to launch my new business, fire my boss, and to pursue my passions full time. At that time, I did not even know what I was passionate about. Now I know it is helping people launch their businesses, fire their bosses, and transform into the best versions of themselves. I have been my own boss for over fifteen years and have both the time and financial freedom to pursue my passions and live the life of my dreams.

Now, I want to do the same for you. In this book, I am going to show you a proven formula that I have used to help train over ten thousand people. You picked up this book because something has happened in your life, and you want to make a change and build the life of your dreams. Are you ready to press the launch button?

ONLY WORKING FOR A PAYCHECK

By society's standards, you most likely are a successful person like I was. You see, I was one of the youngest IT executives for an international media company (Getty Images) that would eventually be sold for $2.2 billion. I was living in a luxury high-rise apartment in Manhattan and making more money than I ever had. I was high on life.

But 9/11 changed all of that. Suddenly, these "accomplishments" did not mean as much to me because I realized I was not passionate about what I was doing. When I experienced the trauma of that day, I was forced out of my comfort zone. Suddenly, I was very aware that I wanted more out of life and that I was only working for a paycheck.

Sometimes major traumas—like the death of a loved one, the end of a relationship, getting laid off (or fired), COVID shutdown, or a near-death experience—have the power to drop-kick us out of our comfort zones and force us to reevaluate life. When that happens, many of us discover we are unhappy and unfulfilled, despite our typical success.

Why? Because we are not following our dreams or passions. We have allowed life to push us around (or into a career) and now feel trapped by it. It is like the waves of the ocean pushing a tree branch around.

"It has been said, most people die at age twenty-five and don't get buried until they are sixty-five. Make an effort to live your life to the fullest."

—LES BROWN

Most people give up on their dreams and long-term goals in their twenties or thirties. They then live the next thirty to seventy years simply going through the motions as "victims of life," all because they gave up on the dreams they wanted when they were young.

If you gave up on your dreams or passions in the past but are reading this book today, it means you have been forced out of your comfort zone and are willing to get back up and try again. Purchasing this book means you have the courage to say, "I want a better life; I want to live the life of my dreams."

Congratulations!

DO YOU STILL BELIEVE THE LIE?

Have you climbed the ladder of success, only to now feel trapped, unhappy, and unfulfilled?

If this is you, you are not alone. Many of the people I work with achieved many levels of "success" and believed their self-worth was tied to their title and how much money they made. They believed the lie.

What is the "lie" I am talking about?

Our entire lives, we have been told a good job will lead to financial freedom. This has been drilled into our heads for decades.

Study hard and get a good education, so you can get a good job.

But this is a lie. Most of us will never experience financial freedom, even if we have a high-paying corporate job. You see, typically, as people make more money, they spend more money to keep up with their new friends' lifestyles. Most of us tend to acquire debt along the way. There is the college loan for a major we picked because we thought we would like one of its corresponding careers. We have no experience in the field but spend the money and take the exams anyway, because we believe it is the right thing to do and will help us accomplish our goals. Unfortunately, it just makes us broke at a higher level.

At some point, we experience something that pushes us out of our comfort zones and makes us realize we have been living a lie. We discover that a steady corporate job does not equate to financial freedom. And for most of us, we realize that it does not make us truly happy and fulfilled, either. As a kid, did you dream of sitting behind a desk all day?

LIVE THE LIFE YOU DESERVE

You are here because you realize you want more out of life and want to build something that you are passionate about. You have been forced out of your comfort zone, and now you want to fire your boss, pave the road to financial freedom, and build the life you deserve.

I was forced out of my comfort zone on 9/11—a lot of us were. I will never forget the things I saw that day or the way I felt. It was traumatic, but it also inspired me to live my dream life.

I have built multiple businesses with multiple income streams. I have flown more than 88,000 miles in one year, which is the equivalent of three and a half trips around the earth. I have had the pleasure of enjoying life while I conduct business:

- in New York City while attending Broadway shows, museums, and live sporting events;

- snorkeling off the beaches in Maui with turtles, seals, and spotted eagle rays;

- staying in three villas overlooking the Adriatic Sea on a small Greek island called Lafkaeda;

- traveling by pirate ship to other Greek islands and private beaches; and

- traveling down the Panama Canal by boat and taking my team snorkeling.

These are just a few of the amazing experiences I have had while building my business. I am passionate about what I do, and I am fulfilled and happy.

This book is designed to teach you to dig deep within and to help you discover your passion. I believe that **Consistent Daily Action** (CDA) leads to success. Therefore, you will need to take action in each chapter of this book to help you find your passion, lay out your goals, and create a plan to launch your business, fire your boss, and more. The goal is for you to leverage the new shared economy model and to be able to work from anywhere in the world using the cash flow from your business and real estate investments (short-term rentals or Airbnb) to support your dream life. You will learn a new perspective on some traditional and creative financing strategies. Build the life you deserve by answering the questions and completing the assignments in each chapter. No matter your current financial situation, you can do it!

Are you ready to press the launch button and build the life you deserve?

I am a no-bullshit person and will tell you exactly how it is, even if you do not want to hear it. If you have a 350 credit score and $500 in the bank, it will likely take you longer to fire your boss and successfully transition out of the corporate world into a more meaningful and fulfilling life. It is still possible. I have faith and firmly believe that anyone can press the launch button and live the life they deserve because I have helped people do it. If you take this seriously, answer the questions, and follow the steps outlined in this book, you too can make your dream life a reality.

THE STAGES TO LAUNCH YOUR BUSINESS AND BUILD THE LIFE YOU DESERVE

You will need to go through several stages to launch your business and build the life of your dreams. The process is similar to that of a rocket launch—planning and preparing, propelling the rocket into space, and then making sure it stays in orbit. This is a great analogy for your business.

Go for Launch or Are You Ready to Launch?

Here is an outline of the stages:

- **Preparing to Launch: Stage 0:** This is the planning and preparation stage. It takes the most amount of time, and if something goes wrong in this stage, you'll never get to launch.

- **Launching Your Business: Stage 1:** The hardest part of a rocket launch is getting the rocket off the ground and into space. That is why the space shuttle has additional booster rockets strapped to it. It needs the extra power from booster rockets to help get it off the ground and break the earth's gravitational pull. It is also the phase where it burns the most fuel. The same is true for launching your business. It will take the most amount of energy and effort to get your business launched and generate the income you desire.

- **Staying in Orbit: Stage 2:** Once a rocket reaches its orbital height, it takes only a little bit of fuel and a few tweaks here and there to keep it in orbit. The same is true for your business. Once it is generating the income you desire, then it takes only a few tweaks to keep it going and enjoy the life you deserve. Are you ready to get started?

THIS WILL NOT BE EASY

I wrote this book to help you find your passion, live a fulfilled and financially free life, but I did not say it was going to be easy!

Along the journey, you will be forced to face some of your fears and overcome them. You will have to let go of things from your past that have held you back from reaching the level of success you deserve. And as you change and grow, you may even lose some friends and/or family members.

Some of you will decide not to finish this book because you will allow life to get in the way. You will stash this book in the back of a drawer or file cabinet and stumble upon it years later. Either that, or the steps outlined in this book will be too hard, and you will choose to quit on your dreams and goals...again. You might read about a third of the book, put it down, and never look at it again.

If this is you, I will tell you the same thing I tell my students: "*You will quit on you before I quit on you.*" Regardless of your journey, if you answer the questions and follow the steps outlined in this book, I will be here for the highs, and I will be here for the lows. Whenever you need a kick in the pants to keep you going, I will be here for that too.

Quitting is the easiest thing you can do. But if you continue to take daily action and never give up on your dreams and goals, you will continue to head down the path toward the life you deserve. You can always quit, so why quit now?

IT TAKES COURAGE

I applaud you because it takes a lot of courage to go against the "lie" or societal norms and decide you want to fire your boss and build your dream. Trust me. I know, because I did it. I needed to make a 180-degree turn after 9/11, and that went against everything we are taught about needing a good job or getting a master's degree and going into more debt. That trauma gave me the courage I needed to eventually launch my business and build the life I deserved.

Over the past fifteen years, I have trained more than ten thousand students. I have taught them how to fire their bosses and live a life of financial freedom. This book is a culmination of all of those trainings. I wrote this book because I believe everyone deserves the chance to live the life of their dreams if they are willing to put in the time and do the work. The concepts I am going to share are not taught in school. I come from three generations of teachers, and this is my way of giving back—to teach adults to think differently, so they can achieve their goals and dreams. I have created a movement called the "eFramily Ohana." Together as a movement, we can enlarge the good we can do in the world. If there are more healthy, happy entrepreneurs working together, we can create amazing things and solve some of the world's problems. But remember, this journey will not be easy. If you complete the assignments in this book and follow the steps I have outlined, you will be able to find your passion, create multiple income streams, and truly live a life of fulfillment. However, God, spirit, the universe, or whatever you believe in (friends and family might do this, too) will likely place obstacles along the way. For the rest of this book, we will call this force or presence "the universe." These are meant to test your willpower and your desire to make your dreams a reality.

"Obstacles do not block the path; they are the path."

—ZEN PROVERB

Change is scary, and this journey will be wrought with fear. Just understand you are being tested to see if you are serious about making a change in your life. If you push past the fear, you will come out on the other side with the dream life you deserve.

As neuroscientist Dr. Joe Dispenza says, "Your brain is a record of the past." It holds you back. However, with more and more practice, those feelings start to go away, and the thing that once scared you becomes your new normal. This is when the magic happens. It is when your entrepreneurial dream life becomes your new reality.

It is important for you to understand where your money philosophy comes from and the Black Swan events that have influenced your life. In the next chapter, we will discuss these philosophies and more.

PREPARING TO LAUNCH
STAGE 0

1

What Is the Black Swan Event That Influences Your Financial Philosophy?

> Your financial philosophy can come from your parents, a person of influence, or even a Black Swan event. Do you know what it is? Either way, are you ready to define it and start the launch sequence to firing your boss?

YOU HAVE ALREADY READ IN THE INTRODUCTION HOW 9/11 took me from being high on life to realizing I needed to make a change to follow my passion. Another factor was the change in corporate politics at my job. You see, as an employee, you do not have control of your financial future unless you have equity in the company you are working for. Even then, you may lose that equity if you leave or are fired from your job.

As an employee, you only have about 5 percent control of your financial future. You have to ask for everything—to come in later, take a long lunch, take time off, or even ask for a raise. Eventually, you reach the glass ceiling where, if you are in the good graces politically, you get the raise, time off, and/or the things you need to run your team.

However, if the politics change, you might find yourself on the outside looking in. This is what eventually happened to me after 9/11. This pushed me towards a path where I ended up making more part time than working my full-time job.

When I say, "fire your boss," I mean you have enough income coming in that you no longer need your income from your job, or you could make more money than by spending forty-plus hours a week at your job. You get to walk into your boss's office and say, "You are fired!"

DO YOU HAVE IT ALL FIGURED OUT?

A lot of people in the corporate world appear as if they have life figured out. My friend Braden once said, "Most people are like puddles. They might be a mile wide but are only an inch deep."

Meaning, they look like they have life figured out on the outside as they climb the corporate ladder, but most are not happy on the inside. They might be killing themselves for their job/company but cannot figure out why they are not happy. They think there is some external stimulant that they need, like a new relationship, promotion, car, etc., that will make them happy.

Most people make themselves so busy and run from thing to thing to avoid looking at themselves. They say things like, "My relationships always go like this." They do not realize that their happiness is an illusion and only temporary.

HAPPINESS IS TEMPORARY

Is this you? If it is, you are not alone. This situation is actually very common. You see, the same thing has happened to me and most of the more than ten thousand people I have coached and trained. We all thought we had life figured out, and then something happened or changed that caused us to realize we were only temporarily happy.

If you are skeptical that happiness is temporary, think about it like this. Look back ten years ago and remember how much money you were making at your job back then. Do you have that number in your head? OK, now would the "old" you from ten years ago be happy with the money you are making today? Over 80 percent of people reading this, as their "old self," would be very happy with their current income. Why are you not happy with the income you are making now?

"Happiness" is a moving target. Once you achieve the thing that you thought would make you happy, it lasts only for a short while, and then the happy feeling goes away and moves on to something else. So, instead of finding happiness, you want to find joy in the process.

THE 50X40X40 TRAP

Another misconception is feeling you cannot change because you are trapped financially at your job. Something that scares people is fear (do not worry, there is a whole chapter later in the book that will go through all the fears), because they feel trapped in their life. You may feel that you have built a life based on a certain income level or status and are trying to keep up appearances with your neighbors and friends. I call this the "50x40x40 trap." What does it stand for?

- **50:** You will work forty-plus hours a week plus your commute, which usually adds up to over fifty hours a week. In the US, we have some of the worst work–life balances in the world.

- **40:** You feel you are supposed to work forty-plus years at a job to qualify for a pension, benefits, and Social Security, or you get nothing.

- **40:** When most people retire, they get to live off of 40 percent of their pay in their golden years.

That does not sound so "golden" to me!

What most people do not realize is that the average person in today's world is actually broke. Most people are only three to five missed paychecks away from going from the penthouse to the outhouse. That is why you need to create a plan to build up income from your side hustle or passion that will eventually replace your salary. I do not want you to fire your boss until you have replaced your income (or can replace your income) with a few more hours dedicated to your side hustle.

Another area of concern for most people is that they do not have any passive income streams built up. They are solely dependent on their salaries to pay their bills and survive. Passive income means that you get paid whether you go to work or not. Now, if you study wealthy people, you will see that the majority of them have owned a business and invested in real estate that generated passive income for them. This means they do not actually have to go to work to make money.

There are many more misconceptions and fears that we will cover later in this book. Here is a list of the top reasons that people fail to become successful.

WHY PEOPLE FAIL TO BECOME SUCCESSFUL

- Taking advice from unsuccessful friends or family

- Being too scared of failure to change and follow their dreams

- Setting goals without a plan to achieve them

- A lack of discipline to follow through

- Not staying consistent in taking daily actions to make their goals or dreams become a reality

- Consistently making excuses for why something cannot be done

- Becoming complacent (stop learning or trying new things)

You know that you should not take advice about how to fix a car's engine from someone who has never driven a car before, right? However, it amazes me that people take business advice from people who have never owned or run a successful business *all the time*. I do not understand why this is. It could be because they are too scared or afraid to follow their dreams, and they want someone to agree with their fears. People come up to me all the time and say they want to make a million dollars. I say great and ask what their plan is to make $1,000 or $10,000 a month first, and they say, "I do not know." A million dollars is a great dream, but if you do not have a plan, then that is all it is. Some people say if you fail to plan, then you are planning to fail.

The real key to changing or learning anything is a CDA and the ability to follow through on an idea. The faster you can go from idea to implementation, the more successful you will be in life. These are two of the key ideas that you have to master to be successful at anything in life. We will discuss these in more detail later in this book. The last two bullet points have to do with allowing yourself to go into victim mode or be comfortable. In cognitive brain therapy, these statements are called **Automatic Negative Thoughts** (ANTs), which our brain produces when we try and do something new. Our society drills being a victim or staying in your comfort zone into our brains. If you are not careful, you will fall into this trap.

"Everything you want is on the other side of fear."

—JACK CANFIELD

I agree with Jack Canfield, but I tell my students, "Everything you want in life is on the other side of fear."

Now that you know some of the common mistakes, we can talk about why you want to take the steps to eject from your job into a new life and find your passion.

WHAT IS YOUR MONEY PHILOSOPHY?

It does not matter where you are currently in life. Instead of doing something that makes you unhappy, you have permission to do a 180-degree turn and follow your passion.

I understand now why my mom and dad made us lunch to take to school each day, and why we always had a coupon when we went out to eat. They needed to make money stretch.

Both of my parents were hard-working teachers who loved to help mold young minds into successful adults. To this day, people in our town still come up to them and thank them for believing in them and helping them to change their lives. They both have wonderful hearts and were involved in the political movements of the sixties, including marching in Washington, DC, with Martin Luther King and other leaders of that era.

On one or two teachers' salaries, however, they struggled financially trying to raise three kids in a middle-class town, in one
of the most expensive areas of the country. They provided a
wonderful home and support for us kids. My mom stopped
teaching when she had me and only went back to teaching when
my younger brother went to nursery school. My dad would typically work a second job every summer and sometimes during the
year so my mom could stay home.

Back then, we called my dad the "coupon king" because you could
only order something at a restaurant if he had a coupon for it. But
I often felt embarrassed at having to pretend to be younger than
I really was so I could order something off the children's menu
for the good of the family. Let me be clear: my parents had great
intentions and wanted to give us the best experiences possible,
but they had to do it on a budget.

They created time freedom, and every few years we would
travel across the country during the summer. We did have to
stay on a budget and make things stretch, but having sixty days
off in a row is great family bonding time. I could tell you more
stories about camping and stopping on the side of the road. As
you can imagine, eating Chef Boyardee ravioli cold out of the
can is awesome. However, sleeping in a tent and swimming in
a cold outdoor pool or taking a cold shower is not a lot of fun!
Have you ever looked back on your life and realized you were a
little poorer than you thought while growing up?

During that same time, I noticed that at family events, my relatives were all staying at nice hotels with indoor, heated pools.
I asked my cousins what their parents did, and they said they

worked in the corporate world. So, I thought that was the solution to becoming financially free. I would go into the corporate world and become wealthy like my relatives. That was my picture of wealth and my financial assumption.

What was your picture of wealth as a kid that became your financial assumption? What is your picture of wealth now?

It does not matter where you are in life. You just have to give yourself permission to follow your passion (or why) and build the life that you deserve. You see, I am just an average guy who did a 180-degree turn when I realized after 9/11 that I wanted more out of life. (I also wrote this book, even though I was told I could not spell, let alone write!) I have helped thousands of people fire their bosses, find their passions, and build the lives they deserve. If my students and I can do it, then you can do it too, but it starts with giving yourself permission to make that 180-degree turn.

Do you give yourself permission?

YOUR FINANCIAL PHILOSOPHY

Now, you need to consider your philosophy about wealth and money. Your current philosophy has been implanted in you by your parents or from watching your parents' actions or their peers. What do I mean?

Our financial beliefs are often implanted in us by our parents, just as their beliefs were implanted in them by their parents, and so on. The financial beliefs of most of our societies go back to the

Great Depression. However, it is no longer the 1920s or 1950s. We need to change that to a 2020s mindset!

Your financial philosophy is made up of your financial discipline and your financial personality. Most people have heard, "money is the root of all evil," or "credit cards are bad." However, money or credit cards do not have personalities. You do not have a "good" credit card that tells you to buy essential things and a "bad" credit card that tells you to buy things you do not need. Money and credit cards just bring out your preexisting financial discipline and financial personality.

Poor and middle-class people are often taught a philosophy of *instant gratification* (the dark circles and arrows in the bottom right of the chart above). They are taught to pay their bills and then hopefully put some money into savings. They save their money and then spend it. They might have even spent it twice and ended up in credit card debt. I bet you know someone who drives around in their net worth and then goes home and sleeps in their parents' basement! That is called instant gratification.

Now, the wealthy teach their kids a different philosophy called *delayed gratification* (the light circles and arrows in the upper left of the chart above). They teach their kids to invest their money in a business and then take the profits from that business and invest in an asset like real estate that generates even more income. They then use that money to get what they want, in essence, for *free*.

This philosophy is how you can get free cars, trips, and college tuition for your kids. How many people wish that their parents understood and taught them this philosophy as a kid?

Not only were your financial habits implanted in you, but your spending habits were as well. As a kid, watching your parents go through certain financial situations influences how you will handle money and finances in the future. You will either follow one of your parents' spending habits, or you will do the exact opposite. Each kid in a household can have very different spending or investing habits because they see experiences from a different perspective or time.

All three of the kids in my family have different spending habits. I tend to take after my dad—I stay on a budget, but I hate to use coupons. My brother is the shopper who will hunt and research a deal for hours and use coupons, and my sister is more of a free spender. Look at your financial philosophy. Do you follow one of your parents' patterns or do the exact opposite? Which parent or adult do you copy or mimic?

WHAT IS YOUR BLACK SWAN EVENT?

You see, not only did we watch our parents' spending habits, but we also watched how our parents handled "Black Swan" events. These major events also have a profound effect on your views on money, debt, and the world.

Black Swan Event

What is a Black Swan event, you ask? You see, back during ancient times in Europe, they used a saying that presumed black swans did not exist because they had never seen one. The Black Swan theory was developed by Nassim Nicholas Taleb. It is defined in summary as:

- The event is a surprise or is so rare that even the possibility that it might occur is unknown.

- The event has a major effect or catastrophic impact when it does occur.

- The event is rationalized or explained afterward as if it *could* have been expected or predicted. Which, of course, it could not.

What Are Some Examples of Black Swan Events?

I already mentioned the Great Depression but a few more recent events that may have shaped your life are the dot-com bubble crash of 2001, 9/11, the US housing crash in 2008, and the coronavirus (COVID-19) pandemic.

These Black Swan events affect people differently depending on when they were born—before 1983, from 1983 to around 2005, or after 2005.

Born before 1983

If you were born before 1983, then most likely your financial mindset is influenced by the Great Depression. You see, a lot of philosophies for building wealth that are passed down from generation to generation come from the Great Depression. Like being able to save your way to wealth, owning the McMansion, relying on your pension to enjoy your golden years, etc. The scary thing is most people nowadays know someone who retired at sixty-five and then had to go back to work and get a second job. They are not enjoying their golden years.

This is a big concern for people getting ready to retire. The question is: will they outlive their money, or will their money outlive them? Someone who is over sixty-five should not be worrying about this. That is why it is important to build both active and passive income from the very start.

Born during 1983–2005

This is the first generation since the Great Depression to grow up in America watching their families struggle financially from too much debt. They watched the stress and anxiety that their parents went through and decided they did not want to take on a lot of debt. Instead, they would rather travel around the world and experience life than invest in large assets and accumulate debt. They want the tiny homes and the freedom to explore the world on the weekends.

This also causes problems because they do not want to take on debt or assets that build long-term wealth.

Born after 2005

It will be interesting to see how people react once everyone adjusts to the "new normal" after our coronavirus quarantine is over. We are still trying to figure out what our new normal will look like, and this will have a big impact on how this generation invests in the future.

I have a few predictions about how things will change. We are already seeing a change in everyone's travel habits. I have been doing a weekly Facebook Live during the COVID pandemic on Wednesdays at 3:00 p.m. EST and will continue doing it afterward. Some of my predictions about how this will change travel and where people will want to travel to in the future are already coming true. So, hop on to my professional Facebook page facebook.com/HughZWealth or on Instagram at @ HughZWealth and click the follow button. Remember to turn the notifications on so you know when I go live.

For taking action and reading this book, go to thelaunchbuttonbook.com/ to get a special bonus report called "The Black Swan." Click on the Black Swan button to register and download the most recent report.

YOU HAVE TO HAVE A SIDE HUSTLE

What most people do not understand is that everyone in today's society should have a side business in case something happens at your full-time job. Then you will still have income plus the tax benefits. This can also act as an income bridge to allow you to follow your passions full time and build the life of your dreams. Your side hustle does not have to be small, like driving for Uber or Lyft. It can be a six-figure income or more.

Most people have heard that starting a new business is risky and that most fail. The opposite is actually true. According to the National Small Business Association's 2017 economic report:

- Eighty percent make it to the second year

- Seventy percent make it to the third year

- Sixty-two percent make it to the fourth year

- Fifty-six percent make it to the fifth year

These statistics do not include businesses that were bought by other companies or situations in which the owner closed and opened a new business, which would push these percentages even higher.

In today's world, I believe *not* having a side hustle or starting a business is actually very risky. We have had several Black Swan events that came out of nowhere to cause an economic crash. Every time, new unemployment claims records were set. This is why you always need to be building a side hustle.

Have you already built your side hustle income or passive income?

THE WEALTHIEST FAMILIES IN AMERICA

If you look at the wealthiest families in America (or in any country around the world), they are business owners and real estate investors. Real estate investing often starts as their side hustle and then becomes worth more than their business. The formula is to own a business and then take the profits from the business to invest in real estate to generate passive income. This is called "use your money twice and then spend it." This is how you get many things in life for free. Remember the diagram from earlier in the chapter?

McDonald's is a great example of this. They no longer are mainly in the hamburger business. McDonald's now owns some of the most expensive real estate in the world, and its real estate assets are worth much more than its hamburger business.

This is a well-proven method that has stood the test of time. Look at the financial histories of the wealthiest families in America, from the Rockefellers and the Vanderbilts to the Walton, Koch, and Mars families.

BUILD ACTIVE AND PASSIVE INCOME

I am a big believer in building both active and passive income. This way, you are not relying on one stream of income and, in essence, putting yourself back into a position of having a job.

I want to make sure we are on the same page moving forward. Therefore, we need to define some terms (in later chapters we will define more technical terms for building a business and real estate investing), but right now, I need you to understand the concept of active versus passive income.

- **Active income** refers to income received from performing a service, such as wages, tips, salaries, commissions, and income from businesses in which there is material participation. For example, an accountant who works for a monthly paycheck receives active income (Kagan 2021).

- **Passive income** is earnings derived from a rental property, limited partnership, or other enterprise in which a person is not actively involved. As with active income, passive income is usually taxable. However, it is often treated differently by the Internal Revenue Service (IRS). Portfolio income is considered passive income by some analysts, so dividends and interest would therefore be considered passive (Chen 2021).

In order to protect yourself during any business, real estate, or market crash, you should have both active and passive income. In my opinion, passive income from real estate is a natural protector for any crash in your entrepreneurial business. There are many ways to use real estate to do this; we will go into it in more detail later in this book. I just wanted to plant the seed that you should be looking to build both active and passive income as you create your plan to fire your boss.

BUILD YOUR SIDE HUSTLE

Ever since I was sixteen, I have had a side hustle. All I wanted to do was play sports, but my parents, being teachers, pushed me toward academics. Math was easy for me, so I was quickly able to adapt to learning about computers. When I turned sixteen, my dad drove me around until I found a job. (I will never forget that.) Even when I was director of technology, I would bartend on the weekends and look for ways to generate extra or passive income. That is how I found my passion—teaching and training entrepreneurs and real estate investors—and it became my side hustle while I was working at my corporate job. Now, it is my full-time gig.

It was not 9/11 that made me cut the umbilical cord connected to my corporate job and push the launch button to fire my boss. It was corporate politics. I was recruited to join Getty Images by one of my old bosses (and friend) who was a director of technology. We had worked together while I was a consultant in IT. I helped him transition through three bank takeovers: from a small five-hundred-person car leasing company to one of the largest banks in the United States. It was one of the easiest and funniest interviews I ever had, and I thought I was golden and set. What no one ever tells you is the closer you get to a C-level position, the more important corporate politics become.

We went through five CTOs at Getty and more VPs of technology. I remember the last new VP of technology at the time. Let's call him Mark. Mark came to New York to talk about moving me and my position to Seattle. He was in New York for four days, and as I showed him our operations and introduced him to our sales directors and VPs, I kept waiting for him to bring up the topic. About an hour before Mark had to leave for the airport, I finally broached the subject with him. I said, "Mark, do you want to talk about moving me and my position to Seattle?" and he reluctantly agreed to talk about it. At that point, I knew something was up and my days were numbered. He had no intention of moving me to Seattle. I did not know it at that time, but a big layoff was coming, and I would have been laid off. Luckily, I had already been working on my side hustle and was making as much money on the side as I was at my corporate job.

The politics at a corporate job, small business, etc., can change quickly, and you can go from being the favorite to the one out of work in a short period of time. What if I had not already been building my side hustle? I would be stressed out having to find another corporate job to keep my lifestyle or try and start a business from scratch. I have found it is always easier to build your side hustle while you have a day job.

That being the case, if you have lost your job or have been fired, sometimes it is a blessing in disguise, because it takes away your safety net. This has happened to some of my students, and they have used it as motivation to build their businesses and invest in real estate.

The most successful entrepreneurs typically have a big why or are very passionate about their business or cause. Let's better define your passion and why in the next chapter.

EXERCISE:
How Do You View Money?

Do you want your answers in a digital format? If so, go to thelaunchbuttonbook.com and click the login button to create your own The Launch Button Blueprint for Success PDF!

Let's define your spending habits, your views on money, and what has shaped your life. This way, we can identify your philosophy for using money. Some of you reading this book will not even realize that you have a money philosophy.

- **What is your Black Swan event?**

_____

_____

_____

- What is your dad's or other male role model's philosophy on money?

  _____

  _____

  _____

- What is your mom's or other female role model's philosophy on money?

  _____

  _____

  _____

- Which philosophy do you follow more closely or do the exact opposite of?

  _____

  _____

  _____

- What is your philosophy on money?

  _____

  _____

  _____

- How do you generate your active income?

_____

_____

_____

- Where does your passive income come from?

_____

_____

_____

- Out of 100 percent...

  * What percentage of your income is active income?

_____

_____

  * What percentage is passive income?

_____

_____

- What are your feelings about debt?

  _____

  _____

  _____

- If you lost your job tomorrow, what is your backup plan?

  _____

  _____

  _____

- What do you want your backup plan to be in the future?

  _____

  _____

  _____

2

Have You Found Your Passion or Your Why?

Your passion, purpose, and why can come from anywhere. Sometimes we just need to listen to the universe and the people around us. Do you know your why, your motivation, or what you are passionate about?

DO YOU KNOW WHICH DAY OF THE WEEK AND AT WHAT TIME most deaths occur in the US? It is Monday before nine in the morning. People are literally dying to go to work. It is either from the stress of another workweek, hating their life of doing the same thing over and over, or a combination of the two. When you are doing something you love, it no longer becomes work. You do not track the number of hours you work in a day or care about staying late or working extra hours. You just do it until it is done. You might even lose all track of time while working on your passion. When you wake up in the morning, it is one of the first things you think about, and you cannot wait to work on building your dream.

The events of 9/11 caused me to reevaluate my passion. Like I said, most people do not know what their passion is. They say things like, "I want to make more money," "I want to have more free time," or "I want to spend more time with family," and so on. But those are not passions. They are surface-level BS answers we tell ourselves. That way, we do not have to really think about our passions. If we did, we might realize that most of us are being pushed or directed through life by society, friends, family, etc., instead of following our dreams or passions. Are you living your dream life or someone else's?

> *"Your time is limited, so don't waste it living someone else's life."*
>
> —STEVE JOBS

To be honest, I was one of those people living someone else's dream life. If you had asked me what my passion was before 9/11, I would not have been able to tell you exactly what it was. I was just following the herd.

WHAT ARE YOU PASSIONATE ABOUT?

My friend Woody Woodward came up with a question: "Besides work and family, what are you passionate about?" I have adopted this question to quickly get to know people. Do you know what most people say? "That is a good question. I will get back to you with an answer." Most people make themselves too busy to sit down and truly figure it out. This is because it forces them to internalize and look at themselves. They cannot blame other people. They must do the work and go inside of their own minds and bodies to figure out what they are passionate about and what would really make them happy. Most people avoid doing the work and would rather float through life like a log on a river. It is so much easier for them to blame other people, life, and so forth, for their current situation.

Often, you know what you are passionate about, but it might be something very simple, and you do not want to admit what makes you happy. Or perhaps it is the opposite: it is really hard to achieve, and you are embarrassed to start the journey. But if you do not know what you are passionate about, here are three great questions to ask yourself:

1. "What am I really good at?"

2. "What do I enjoy doing?"

3. "What do people keep coming to me for help with?"

Whichever the case, once you make the decision to follow your passion or your path to happiness, the universe and the doors of life will magically start to open for you.

LISTEN TO THE UNIVERSE

Sometimes the universe is telling us to do things that we know we should do, but we keep putting them off.

> Remember, you can replace universe with God, spirit, or whatever you believe in. I am just going to call it "universe" to keep it simple for the rest of the book.

Often, you just need to shut up and listen to the universe. Instead, we try and fight this plan that keeps popping up in our minds.

Usually, it is because we are afraid that we are going to fail. It can be scary to do a 180-degree pivot to a new career, or we might look bad to friends and family. If we do not listen to the universe, the messages just keep repeating. Or worse, we continue to experience the same "learning mistakes" over and over again.

I do not call them failures, and I will explain that in later chapters. We want to get through as many learning mistakes as possible and as quickly as we can. To do this, we must be brave enough to listen and see the signs the universe gives us and be willing to take the necessary actions to follow the path, even if it appears scary. And it will *always* appear scary in the beginning.

"The scariest moment is always just before you start."

—STEPHEN KING

There are signs all around us. The question is: have you been listening to the signs from the universe or blocking them out? What thoughts, opportunities, or things keep popping up in your life? If the universe wants you to learn it, do it, and so on, then there is a good reason for you to do it. One of the best ways to find your passion is to experience new things. Who knows, it may become your new passion in life. Stop fighting it and start embracing the opportunities in front of you.

You have permission to follow your heart, your passion, your dreams, and your goals. When you do, you will start to live a more fulfilled life and find joy all around every day. This does not mean you should quit your job and open a tiki bar on a small island somewhere. It means it is time to start taking action to build your dream life.

This is going to be one of the scariest things you have ever done. Let me explain.

ONE OF THE SCARIEST THINGS I'VE EVER DONE

Writing this book is one of the scariest things that I have ever done. You see, the story in my head for over thirty years was that I am not a writer, and I know I suck at spelling and grammar. The Oxford comma and I did not get along. I never did well in English class and writing compositions, so how could I ever write a book?

(Do not worry. We will talk about all your fears and the naysayers in your life and how to overcome them on your entrepreneur journey in Chapter Five. Trust me...I have gone through just

about every fear and situation possible and have coached students through theirs on their entrepreneur journeys.)

I was too scared to do it myself back in 2007/2008, so I hired a ghostwriter. We got four or five chapters done, but it was being written in the wrong voice. Shortly thereafter, the real estate market crashed, and it no longer made sense to pay him to write the book at that time.

Fast-forward to early 2019. I was talking with a friend who had recently written an Amazon top-selling book on investing in real estate and he said, "You know so much more than I do about real estate investing. You know you should write a book, right?" I said, "I know," but I blew it off because of my fear of writing and the negative experience I had had with the ghostwriter.

About a month later, I was sitting at my local bar in New York City, and a young professional woman came in and sat next to me to eat dinner. She worked for a wealthy investor—she helped him run his charities and edit his books. She wanted to buy a property but being from Australia, she did not fully understand how our financial system worked. I explained some of the basic financial concepts and things she could do to put herself in a better position to qualify to buy a property.

She said, "You know, you should write a book about this, right?" I once again said, "I know." However, I again quickly dismissed the idea.

I flew to Utah for a day of training with one of my mentors. As part of laying out the plan for a new company that I was launching, I told him my why and my story.

He said, "You know you have to write a book about this, right?"

This person is a *New York Times* bestselling author.

Again, I said, "I know." Finally, I got the message that the universe was trying to tell me. It was time for me to shut up, stop making excuses, and give myself permission to write this book.

After that day, do you know what has happened? The words flowed out of me every time I sat down to write. It did not matter where I was—the middle of Las Vegas, New York City, Toronto, or sitting on a beach in Panama City, Panama. The only thing I wanted to work on was writing my book. The guy who hated to write, could not spell, and was barely ever grammatically correct only wanted to sit down and write his book each day.

Once you find your passion (or give in to your passion) and allow it to flow, you will want to work on making your passion a reality and building your dream life. What has the universe been telling you to do?

FINDING MY PASSION

My job was OK, but it was not something that I was passionate about. To be honest, I do not think I was ever passionate about computers or IT. In middle school, when computers first came out, I became good at programming and then stayed on that path. People told me I should get my master's in computer science so I could make more money. I took two master-level courses, but it did not change how I felt. I was living everyone else's dream and not my own.

I read *Rich Dad, Poor Dad* by Robert T. Kiyosaki and a few other real estate investor books, but I still was not sure what I wanted to do. I decided while I was figuring things out that I was going to buy a property with two bedrooms. I could then rent out a bedroom so someone else would help me pay off my mortgage, and I could start to build passive income.

I did not really know that much about investing in real estate or how to do it. I should have taken a training program, but I thought since I read a few books, I could figure it out by myself. Back then, there was not internet access to quality training programs, coaches, or mentors to help guide you through the process. I wasted a lot of time and money trying to do it on my own.

Living in Manhattan, there were only a few types of properties I could buy—a **condo**, **co-op**, or a **cond-op**. If you do not ever have to deal with co-ops, then you are lucky. In a co-op, you own shares in a building, and everything needs to get board approval. Co-op boards can legally discriminate against anyone. A cond-op has many variations and is a combination of a co-op and a condo.

I decided early that I wanted to buy a condo in New York City, even though it would be more expensive. I wanted to be able to rent out a spare bedroom and I did not want someone telling me what I could and could not do in my own home or in the future. As I mentioned above, I made a lot of mistakes on my first real estate deal, such as:

- I hired the wrong agent because she lived on my floor (neighborhood).

- I did not fully read my mortgage paperwork and got stuck with a bad interest rate and fees.

- I did not get the construction changes that the seller had agreed to make to my condo in writing.

These mistakes cost me both time and money.

The *only* thing I did right was find a building going through a condo conversion from rent-controlled to condo. They had to sell 10 percent of the units before they could apply for approval to become an official condo in New York City. They needed to sell their units fast and had them listed $50,000 below market value. I saw an opportunity, acted quickly, and signed a contract. It was supposed to take three to four months to convert the building, but it took about six months before I was finally able to close on the deal. At that point, the property had already appreciated another $50,000. So, even with all of my mistakes, I was already profitable.

After closing on my first real estate deal, however, I still was not passionate about being an entrepreneur or a real estate investor. Buying a property made me realize there were other ways to make money. I was curious to learn more, and once you give yourself permission to start looking around for other opportunities, you start to see them everywhere.

This is called activating your **Reticular Activating System** (RAS). More on that in a moment.

WHAT IS MY PASSION?

I love training people and watching the light bulbs go off above my students' heads as they learn new sales, communication, speaking, financial, or real estate concepts. I enjoy watching them apply these concepts to their lives. Maybe it is the three generations of teachers in me, but for me this impact is priceless. I have proudly trained:

- A twenty-two-year-old high school dropout who is now making over $100,000 a year as a part-time real estate investor and entrepreneur.

- A female military veteran who was injured and has now completed just shy of one hundred transactions, buying most properties with only $10 down and making over $250,000 as a real estate investor in a year.

- An eighty-three-year-old retired author who completed her first fix and flip and is building her business and personal credit while finding gratification.

I could rattle off thousands of stories about my students who have learned how to apply new skills, build passive income, fire their boss, and enjoy the life they deserve. It gives me goose bumps just writing about the success of my students!

I am also a serial entrepreneur. That is my second passion. I love building businesses, running numbers, and applying creative financial strategies to real estate deals. For me, it is like playing Tetris, doing a crossword puzzle, or solving a Rubik's Cube. I cannot do any of those other things, but I can come up with opportunities to start a business to fill a need. I can structure a creative strategy in my head to make it a win for the seller, my partners, and me. This also becomes a win for the future buyers and/or lenders usually within a few hours on a real estate deal or business opportunity.

You see, I activated my brain's RAS and it led me to find my true passion. Are you ready to activate yours?

Anthony "Tony" Robbins was the first to introduce this system before the turn of the century. The RAS is the filter that your brain uses to filter the over two million bits of information that your senses receive daily. The RAS essentially "decides for you" exactly what you will consciously give your attention to at any given moment. A perfect example is when you buy a new car; you begin to see that same car everywhere. These cars were there all along, but your brain just was not paying attention to them. Now, you never know where your passion will come from. People say the best way to find it is to try new things that you are curious about. You should experiment with new ideas or just say yes to life and keep your eyes open for opportunities. This is how the universe helps open your eyes to your passions and possibilities.

ACTIVATE YOUR BRAIN'S RAS

Another example of my RAS kicking into gear happened a few months later. I was invited to a college friend's wedding in North Carolina, and I planned to drive down with three friends, but only two of us ended up going. Mike and I ran out of things to talk about by the time we hit Delaware, with another seven-plus hours to go.

Activating Your Brain's RAS

Who knew that going to a wedding in North Carolina would change my life?

Neither of us had ever been to Myrtle Beach. We had planned to stay at our friends' place that night and then drive the last two hours the next day. After we arrived, we needed to talk to other people (at that point, anyone would do!), so we went out for dinner. I happened to pick up a local real estate guide and saw how cheap the property prices were compared to places in NYC, and I became curious about the area and its interesting beach town.

Before I could investigate why everything in this area was so cheap, we had to drive to the wedding in Wrightsville. The event was held at a small local hotel near the beach. As we pulled into the parking lot of the hotel, I noticed it looked more like a motel. We were definitely not in NYC anymore! We checked in and went straight to our own rooms to drop off our stuff, freshen up, and get ready for the prewedding festivities. When I walked into my hotel room, I could tell there was something different. My unit was decorated in an ocean theme with a king bed. I walked over to Mike's room, and his was decorated with a totally different theme and a queen bed. I thought this was odd because we both booked the same type of hotel room. Why would his décor and bed size be so different?

We walked back down to the front desk to get some recommendations. I asked, "Does each room have a different theme?" The clerk said, "Yes, this is a condo hotel. Each unit has a different owner, and they decorate them however they want. As well, they have the right to stay there whenever they want." I never knew something like this existed. You do not know what you do not know.

Once you open up your brain's RAS, ideas and opportunities will form that lead you to your passion. What if I could buy a property in a warm beach location much cheaper than in NYC and be able to generate passive income when I was not using it? I thought this was a brilliant idea, and I needed to learn more about condo hotels. Were there a lot more of them? How did they work?

When I got back to New York, I started learning everything that I could about them. Jeff, one of my college friends who was also at the wedding, was interested in investing in real estate. So, we teamed up. We thought we had hit a gold mine and started investing. Some of our properties doubled in value in less than a year.

Jeff is a little older than me and was a lot wiser at that time. He wanted to sell some of the units, but I wanted to hold them and build long-term wealth. Unfortunately, we got hit hard with the Black Swan event of the 2008–2010 real estate crash. I definitely learned a lot of lessons during that crash...the hard way.

Shortly after we started investing in condo hotels, I realized I would need to raise more capital for deals and make better presentations to higher-level investors. I saw an ad in a magazine for a training on how to make presentations and become a public speaker. This was exactly what I was looking for. I immediately signed up and paid for the "Professional Speakers' Boot Camp." I did such a good job presenting at the boot camp that the company giving the presentation offered me an opportunity to fly around the country to teach and train people how to invest in real estate. (More details on this story later.) At the time, I did not even know there was an industry out there that taught people how to invest in real estate. I said yes to the opportunity and it led me to replace my director of technology income by working part time training people and investing in real estate. I was able to fire my boss back in 2005. I have not had a real job since.

"Always say 'yes' to the present moment... Surrender to what is. Say 'yes' to life—and see how life starts suddenly working for you rather than against you."

—ECKART TOLLE

Do you see how the universe led me down a path because I kept saying yes to life and to finding my passion? Once you say yes to one opportunity, you never know where it will lead you. Who knew saying yes to attend a wedding in North Carolina and continuing to say yes to opportunities could lead me to find my passion, fire my boss, and launch my new life?

DISCOVERING YOUR WHY

Do you know your why?

When I ask most people this question, they do not know what really drives them. They are too busy being busy or going through the motions of life. So, we are going to take time now to start the deep dive into your why. You may not find it right away with this exercise, and that is OK. What this exercise is meant to do is help you start thinking about it. By the time you finish reading this book, you should have a clear understanding of your why.

It usually takes a big or small trauma in your life for you to want to make a change. It could be something with your job, your relationship, family, etc. that causes you to stop and want to reevaluate your life. For me, it was 9/11.

Why do you want to launch out of your current job, situation, or lifestyle?

- Did you have a major life change or trauma?

- Do you want to pursue your passion?

- Are you ready to be your own boss?

- Are you dissatisfied with your job or with corporate America?

- Did an opportunity present itself?

- Do you feel you deserve more out of life and want to build the life you deserve?

- Are you *not* ready to retire?

- Something else?

You probably are unhappy or not satisfied at your job. You want more in your future, but you are not sure exactly how to get there or you do not know your why. Well, the easiest way to find your why and get there is to just start saying yes to life and the opportunities around you. You see, there are opportunities all around you. You just have to stop *thinking* and start *doing* it. These opportunities might appear to be scary but that is OK. You will be surprised how the universe starts leading you in a direction to find your why once you start saying yes.

> Everything you want in life is just on the other side of fear. All you need is five seconds of courage to go for it!

Why do you want to make the change? For now, you just have to recognize that you are ready to change your path and start the journey.

EXERCISE: Find Your Why

Do you want your answers in a digital format? If so, go to thelaunchbuttonbook.com and click the login button to create your own The Launch Button Blueprint for Success PDF!

- **What is your why for making a change?** Which reason(s) listed above is why you want to press the launch button and escape from your current situation? A genuine why will prevent you from quitting on your dreams or goals. It is easy to keep moving toward those goals and dreams when things are going well. But what is going to keep you going when life knocks you down, and you have to get back up and try again?

  _____

  _____

  _____

- What are five reasons you will not quit and give up on your goals or dreams when life knocks you down?

  _____

  _____

  _____

  _____

  _____

- What are your top five priorities in life?

_____

_____

_____

_____

_____

- Now, look at your list of priorities. Are they what you spend most of your time doing? Or do you need to change how you spend your time?

_____

_____

_____

_____

_____

Now, let's get clear and find your passion.

EXERCISE:
What Are You Passionate About?

Do you want your answers in a digital format? If so, go to http://thelaunchbuttonbook.com/ and click the login button to create your own The Launch Button Blueprint for Success PDF!

What are you passionate about?

It is scary that most people do not know what they are passionate about because they never thought about it before. So, here is an exercise to help you find your passion or your why.

Take five minutes and think about what has kept reappearing in your life that you need to do, learn, or follow through on.

1. What do you do that makes you lose track of time and yourself? Or what do you love to do?

2. What do you spend money on that you love to do?

3. What are some things you do or hobbies that you are afraid to tell other people about? (You might be afraid that they are going to judge you for doing them.)

4. What makes your heart race when you do it?

On a piece of paper, create three columns:

- **Column 1:** What are some things that you are curious about?

- **Column 2:** What problems do you like to or want to solve?

- **Column 3:** What is something *new* you always wanted to try or place to travel to?

Write down at least ten responses in each column.

Now, look at your answers from all of these questions and the questions above. Do you see items that are similar or grouped around a topic? Do you see one answer that you are really excited about? If so, you have found your passion.

If you still have not found it, that is OK as well. Sometimes we just need to activate our RAS and it starts working in our subconscious to find the answer over the next couple of weeks. Pick one of your answers and start researching or solving it for a week and see if it sparks your passion. If not, then move to your next answer.

Once you find it, it is time to say yes to life and start taking CDA on your passion.

3

Do You Have the Right Skills?

Learning Financial Skill

> Be confident and willing to ask for help in areas where you know you need to learn or improve. This will help you realize your dream business.

DEPENDING ON YOUR PASSION, YOU MAY NEED TO LEARN A new skill or a *few* new skills. You may also need to learn some business, marketing, sales, and leadership skills. Your background and life experiences have helped you develop many skills, and you will just need to fill in the gaps. This may be hard because you may suck at some of them in the beginning but that is OK. You do not have to be a master in each category, but you will need to put in some time to improving your own skills and knowledge.

There is one skill every successful entrepreneur needs to possess in order to get people excited, and it is transferable without any training. Do you know what it is? It is called excitement. Other people will feed off your excitement. This positive energy inspires people to get behind your cause. No one wants to follow a lethargic, monotone person. Get excited and show everyone your passion! You will then watch people line up to follow you. Passion, excitement, and consistency beat skill and talent each and every day.

The great thing is everything you have done in your life (right or wrong) has prepared you for this moment. These "learning lessons" prepare you for your future. I call them "learning lessons" (as opposed to failures), because we tend to learn more from our mistakes than we do our successes. Some people feel they do not have anything to get started with, but we all have some resources or capital at hand. Here is a list of some you may already have:

- Money

- Time

- Real Estate

- Entrepreneurship/Business

- Relationships

- Physical Health

- Mental Health

- Personal Financing

- Credit

You probably have one or several of these already lined up for you. However, there is usually one or two you will need to improve upon to achieve your goals and dreams. Which one is the most valuable for your future success?

Depending on where you are in life, they are all important. However, there is only *one* we can never get back. When you are lying on your deathbed, you are not likely to say, "I wish I had more money." The only one we cannot get back is *time*. I am going to make sure I value your time while you read this book and build the life you deserve.

One of the best exercises to get a solid understanding of your-self and the skills you need to learn is to do a **SWOT analysis**. A SWOT analysis is a way for you to understand your **s**trengths, **w**eaknesses, **o**pportunities, and **t**hreats as you start to build the life of your dreams. I will walk you through this exercise at the end of the chapter.

ARE YOU READY TO INVEST IN YOU?

When seeking a new profession or skill, people often feel paying for this knowledge is a scam. Why is that? These same people will pay $100,000-plus and go into debt for a college education they may never use. A college education, most of the time, does not teach you basic financial knowledge or even business skills. Would you let me operate on your brain knowing I had no training or education in brain surgery? I would hope the answer is no. However, I have seen many, many people try to start a business or invest in real estate without any training or education. Then after losing $20,000 to $100,000, they wonder why they have failed to reach their goal and lost their life's savings.

There are three ways to learn something without going back to college:

1. The School of Hard Knocks.

2. Buy a training, coaching, or mentorship program.

3. Volunteer, serve, or work out a trade of services for free mentoring. (Always serve first and then after you have been serving for a while ask for guidance or mentorship.)

The second option is the fastest and safest way to learn. I call it "borrowing someone else's brain." It saves your most precious asset: time. As I mentioned earlier, you do not know what you do not know. I feel it is cheaper to learn from other people's mistakes than bang your head against the wall making the same mistakes all over again. Coaches, mentors, trainers, and education from experienced people is the fastest way to learn. They have years of experience to help you avoid the problems you do not even know exist. I love to "borrow the brains" of people who have already gone through or dealt with the things that I am about to. This may require paying them for training.

> *"The most important investment you can make is in yourself."*
>
> —WARREN BUFFETT

Most wealthy and highly successful people constantly invest in training, seminars, and/or mentors each year to learn a new skill or help take an area of their life to the next level. Why is it that most poor and middle-class people think it is a scam to invest in these trainings or seminars? It is important to understand the areas or skills you need to learn in order to become successful in the future. The most important investment you can make is in yourself and in your knowledge.

CREATE A FRICTIONLESS PROCESS TO LEARN FASTER

You can save $10,000 to $100,000 and weeks, months, or years of time just by learning from other people's mistakes and hiring coaches/trainers/mentors. These professionals see the world differently because of their life experiences and their own "learning lessons." Their thought processes have changed over time based on those experiences. This saves you time and money.

It often makes sense to pay for the opportunity to train with a mentor. I learned early on to use coaches and mentors to learn faster and paid over $20,000 for one single day to train with a mentor. The return on that day has doubled in value in connections alone. The other way I have gotten valuable training from mentors is by bringing or doing something of value for them first. I have always been able to master bringing value to people who are doing what I want to be doing in the future. The one thing you never want to do is waste that person's time or argue with them.

If coaches/trainers/mentors ask you to do something, do not hesitate or question them; just do it. Once you have completed the task, you may understand why they had you do it. If not, the appropriate time to ask them is now, after you are done. Just remember Daniel and Mr. Miyagi from *The Karate Kid*. If you make it a frictionless process, they will take you under their wing and show you the ropes. This will also help you build trust with them and let them know they can count on you to get the task done. Coaches/trainers/mentors want to invest their time in people who are eager to learn and willing to take action. Remember, their most valuable asset is time, and they do not like to waste it. A mentor can save you a lot of money, because you will be learning from their mistakes. This is the fastest way to learn.

HOW MENTORS SAVED ME TIME AND MONEY

There are no shortcuts to success, but let me share a couple of my personal experiences about how mentors and trainers have saved me time and money.

From a Magazine Ad to Six Figures Part Time

Shortly after starting my real estate investing business, I realized I needed to learn how to create effective presentations to be able to raise more capital from people to invest in my deals. I had given presentations in business to CTOs, SVPs, and Wall Street analysts to get millions of dollars for IT projects, but I had never asked someone to give me a million dollars before.

I was reading a magazine and I saw an ad for a three-day boot camp on how to become a public speaker. You know the ones you usually laugh at and say to yourself, "It is too good to be true." Whenever the universe offers you something that is 70–80 percent of what you want, you must say yes and do it. I immediately knew this was what I needed. I would have to take one day off from working at Getty to attend this three-day boot camp, but I could learn how to raise capital and build my own training program. The number one fear for most people is speaking in public. I always say, "More people would rather be in the coffin than giving the eulogy." However, I knew I had to conquer this fear to raise capital, so I paid for and signed up for the boot camp.

When I walked into the boot camp, I was surprised by how small the class was. There were only eight paying students but seven people from the training company. There were a variety of people in the class—a woman who wanted to teach pole dancing, another woman who wanted to teach an AA-like program, and only one other businessperson from corporate America. Everyone needs to learn how to speak in public. Most people do not realize that the person giving the presentation is the one who makes the most money or gets the most recognition, no matter their profession or industry.

Over the first two days, we were given a lot of great information on inflection, pacing, presenting, and setting up a room, and we gave several practice presentations. At the end of day two, we were offered the ability to buy a $4,995 coaching program. This would allow us to develop our presentation skills to give our own trainings in the future. I was seriously considering this because I wanted to raise capital and build a solid presentation for my future investors.

Before I even left the room, a lady walked up to me and said, "I would like to talk to you about a potential opportunity to train real estate investors nationwide." She asked me to stick around, and I said, "OK." I was curious to learn how I could get paid to train investors and raise capital at the same time.

She said, "Hi, my name is Edna. I like the way you presented during class, and I would like to offer you an opportunity to speak and train for our company." At the time, I did not know there was a whole industry of professional speakers and trainers. Many trainers flew around the country teaching people different subjects like real estate investing, entrepreneurship, self-improvement, and motivation. Edna managed all the public speakers and trainers for the company providing the boot camp.

There was an element of sales in the job, and I explained I had never done sales before. She said, "You are a natural trainer." She went on to explain the position and what it would entail. What she was actually offering was a five-week "tryout" with training. If I made it through the tryout, then they would give me the opportunity to speak for the company all across the country. She added that she only hired speakers who had experience, so if I bought the coaching program and gave a presentation for the magazine, she would hire me. I said, "Thank you for the opportunity. Let me think about it, and I will let you know tomorrow." I still had homework to do to develop my training presentation for the last day of the boot camp.

When I got home that night, I went through the pros and cons of the opportunity.

PROS	CONS
I would be able to build my presentation skills quickly with the additional training program.	I would have to buy the additional training program.
I would get additional training from top-flight speakers.	I would have to stop bartending in the Hamptons (my fun job).
I could quickly build a network of real estate professionals and investors.	If I did not make it through the five-week tryout, I would be let go.

However, since I still had my IT job with plenty of PTO (paid time off), there really was not any risk in my mind. So I decided to say yes to life and go for it.

The power of learning a new skill can create a new career associated with your passion.

I never thought that purchasing a training program and learning a new skill would change my life forever, but it did. This new public speaking skill opened up a whole new world of opportunities for me. I went from the newest instructor out of over forty trainers to being the fourth-most revenue-producing instructor in the entire training division in just one year. I was making more money working part time as a speaker than I was at my full-time IT job.

Everything that you have been exposed to in your life is preparing you for the rest of your life. Sometimes, we do not see it as we go through the ups and downs. But let me explain further.

BRING VALUE TO THE BEST
OF THE BEST

"Read 500 pages like this every day. That's how knowledge works. It builds up, like compound interest. All of you can do it, but I guarantee not many of you will do it."

—WARREN BUFFETT

The five-week speaking program was not easy. I was sent to different cities around the US to learn the company's presentations and be trained by seasoned speakers on the weekends. Then I would fly back on red-eyes and work my IT job during the week. However, I was determined to make it work. For the first two weeks, all I did was take notes for eight hours a day. After the students left, I gave a one-hour presentation to the speakers for practice. On week three, I was sent out with the number one team to be trained by Mike and Ted. They consistently produced the best sales numbers and were given the largest cities and biggest events to train students. I was ready to learn from the best of the best.

I was not the only one in training that week with Mike and Ted. There was another instructor in training named Angela, and she was further along in the training program. They would have Angela get up and present some sections so both Mike and Ted could talk one-on-one with students.

Throughout the weekend, I was trying to listen in on Mike and Ted's conversations with students to learn their secrets. I was so new, I did not know this was called "overcoming objections." They did not like the fact that I was listening to their conversations—we had not built any rapport. They did not know what to make of this guy from New York City.

After they caught me listening in on a few of their one-on-ones, they decided to give me some of the students who would be hard sells and felt did not have the money to buy the training program. They were trying to keep me busy and to stop me from listening in on their conversations. I was nervous but figured this would be good practice for me. One of the students was a teacher looking to change careers and become an entrepreneur and real estate investor. Coming from three generations of teachers and understanding the financial struggle they go through, I could really relate to her. We talked for fifteen minutes (or so) and I helped her come up with a plan to buy the training program she wanted.

I did not even know how to fill out the order form to get her started. I walked over to Mike and Ted while they were in the middle of another one-on-one. They looked annoyed as I approached.

I said, "Excuse me, she wants to buy the program."

They looked at me in disbelief and Ted said, "What do you mean?"

"We came up with a plan for her to buy the training program. How do I fill out the order?"

Ted looked at me and said, "Well, alright then!"

He excused himself from the conversation, walked me back to my table, and helped the student fill out her paperwork. After that, I was golden with Mike and Ted. I brought them value by generating income for them and helping them become the top instructors that weekend. They also realized I would do what they wanted in a frictionless manner.

For the rest of my training program, they requested I work with them. Since they were the top sales team and trainers in the company, they got what they wanted. I soaked up everything I could from them and was hired full time after my five-week training program.

I really learned the psychology and strategy for making effective presentations from Mike and Ted. Those lessons and golden nuggets have allowed me to raise millions of dollars in capital and make good money each year as a speaker and trainer.

Who would have thought that paying for a training program would lead me to a new career as a public speaker and entrepreneur as well as a full-time real estate trainer and investor? I also get to travel the country and write these business expenses off my taxes. It was not easy, but I took consistent daily action and did the work. Now, I get to do what I want, when I want.

> **Bonus:** The company that trained me has closed, but I have recreated a similar speakers' boot camp. I now train people on ways to become a public speaker and build their own training programs. Many have gone on to make over six figures and raise millions in capital for their deals. If you want to learn more about it, then go to hughzaretsky.com/start-here.

GIVE YOURSELF PERMISSION TO SUCK

I need you to understand that you are going to suck at some of the new things you will learn or try to do. That's OK. You need to give yourself permission to suck. Somehow as adults, we think we need to be good at everything we try. Let's be real—that is not always the case. I tell my team, "I need you to give yourself permission to suck and then get better." The best way to learn is by experimenting and trying new things. Joe Madden used this strategy with the Chicago Cubs, and they were able to win their first World Series in over one hundred years.

Think about it like this: the first time a baby tries to walk, what happens? They will fall down 99.9 percent of the time. When that happens, you do not tell the baby to stay down and crawl for the next three to five years, right? No, you make sure the baby is OK and then encourage them to try again.

This is common sense, right? Why then, as adults, when we try our hand at an entrepreneurial business, real estate investing, or something else and fail, do we bury our heads and go back to our jobs? Most people do not try again for another three to five years. You need to have the courage to pick yourself up, dust yourself off, and try again. Just like the baby, if you fail enough times and learn from those failures, then you will eventually succeed by not only walking, but by running towards success.

> *"Defeat is a state of mind; no one is ever defeated until defeat is accepted as a reality."*
>
> —BRUCE LEE

This is why you need to give yourself permission to suck and then get better. I always say, "Fail fast and fail forward." We actually learn more from our mistakes than our successes.

Now that you have given yourself permission to suck and to learn new skills, let's do a SWOT analysis or self-evaluation of where you are and what skills you need to learn in the future to reach your goals. Once you understand this, you can find mentors or training programs that will speed up your learning process, like I did.

EXERCISE:
SWOT Analysis

Do you want your answers in a digital format? If so, go to thelaunchbuttonbook.com and click the login button to create your own The Launch Button Blueprint for Success PDF!

This self-evaluation is a great exercise for you to do about you. You then want to do the exercise a second time about the business you want to start or build bigger.

As a refresher, SWOT stands for strengths, weaknesses, opportunities, and threats. Strengths and weaknesses are internal factors you can control. Opportunities and threats are outside forces you do not initially have control over.

Strengths (Internal)

- What do you do well?

- What qualities separate you from other people or your competitors?

- What experiences do you have that give you an edge over your competition?

- What are your areas of expertise or skills?

- What resources (intellectual property, technology, etc.) give you an edge?

Weaknesses (Internal)

- In which areas of life or business do you need to improve?

- What qualities do your competitors have that you need to improve?

- What additional experience do you need to gain?

- Who are the contacts that you need to build a better relationship with to reach your goal?

- What additional resources do you need?

Opportunities (External)

- Who needs you or your product/services?

- What emerging market is underserved that you or your product/services can fill the need for?

- How can you generate more recognition, press, or media coverage for you or your product/services?

- Are there any new social media or technology trends that can help you grow?

- What additional training(s) can you take to grow yourself and your business?

- What organizations or people can you network with to expand your reach?

Threats (External)

- What is the biggest risk to your plan for success?

- What emerging trends can affect your plan of action?

- What technology changes may disrupt your plans?

- Are there any regulations or changes in the law that could affect your business?

- Which customer-changing attitudes could affect your business?

- What obstacles could prevent you from reaching your goals?

Now, remember to repeat this exercise for your business idea. If you do not have one yet that is fine. This book will spark a bunch of ideas for you and will help you develop them. Just remember to come back to this exercise after you have developed your business idea and redo the exercise.

4

Permission to Go against the Norm!

Breaking down your conventional versus nonconventional thoughts about being an entrepreneur, business owner, and real estate investor.

As you set off on your entrepreneur and real estate investor journey, you will be going against the norm of society, and there will be many social and internal pressures that you will have to overcome. You are going to have to create your "new normal," and it is going to keep changing over time. You will want to quit many times throughout this process, and that is OK. I always say, "Quitting is easy and you can do it at any time, so why quit now?" Just take one more action, make one more phone call, do one more thing, and *that* is usually when you will find success. The hardest thing to do in life is to keep going when it feels like everyone and everything is against you. All of these obstacles keep appearing, and your brain wants you to quit. These ANTs want to keep you where you are in life. It is *really* f-ing *hard* to stay focused and push through them. Every successful entrepreneur has had to conquer these fears and keep going.

The harsh truth is your brain has gotten you to your current financial situation or place in the world. If you want to be in a different place, then you need to start listening to someone else's brain.

Humans are the only living organisms in the world who can *choose* not to live up to their full potential. A tree will never decide to grow to only half of its natural height. A tree's roots will push and burrow as deep as possible through rocks and anything else that stands in its path to spread out and find water. A tree will grow as tall as it possibly can towards sunlight and will allow the maximum number of leaves on each of its branches. Never would a tree "not feel" like having leaves on a certain branch or decide to stop growing. However, as humans, we have the freedom of choice. A lot of people choose to not reach their full potential. They settle into their lives or their current situations because their thoughts hold them back.

Depending on where you are in life, this is a result of the thoughts implanted on you as a kid and/or through your own experiences. Dr. Joe Dispenza, a chiropractor whose postgraduate work includes neuroscience and epigenetics, says, "Our brain is a record of the past, not the future." When we do things that are outside of the "normal" for our brain, such as learning something new, taking a risk on a relationship, investing, or launching a business, this ALWAYS makes our brains feel uncomfortable. That is why we will have the emotional swings, thoughts about quitting, and going back to our old habits, relationships, or job. We need to push through those thoughts and realize they are just trying to hold us back. I tell people, "You need to stop listening to your brain and listen to someone else's brain if they are where you want to be." If that person tells you to do something, then do it and do not think about it. Remember the frictionless process from the last chapter? Eventually, these new tasks, actions, thoughts, etc. will become your new normal, and the fear will pass.

Most people think there is a smooth, straight line to success. I see a lot of entrepreneurs who try to go from zero to millionaires overnight and end up quitting in frustration. This is because they only see famous people, or a superstar, after they have become a finished product. They do not see all of that person's failures or years of hard work behind the scenes.

> You cannot go from zero to hero. You will need to stairstep your way to success.

You still have to take steps each day to reach your goal. I tell my students all the time that CDA beats skill every day of the week. In the beginning, these actions may not produce results. It might be as little as buying a domain name, reading a book, listening to a podcast, signing a lease, etc. CDA compounds over time, allowing you to reach your goals. To stairstep your way to success, you need to break down your goals into smaller actionable steps.

Most people create long to-do lists, and even when they accomplish a task, they feel unproductive because they have a lot more items on their list, and it seems like an uphill battle. Most people put things off, or they get distracted by life and avoid taking action towards their goals. It is CDA that leads to success. Eventually CDA will compound over time and take off exponentially.

My book *Steps to Fire Your Boss—5 Week Productivity Journal*, allows entrepreneurs to stairstep their way to success because it helps them focus on completing their "three big tasks" for the day. Once my team started using it, they felt like they were successful and moving closer to their goals and dreams. They even got more items completed because they were confident and on a roll.

(Get your own copy of the *5 Week Productivity Journal* at: hughzaretsky.com/books.)

IT'S NOT MAGIC, IT'S CDA THAT MAKES PEOPLE GREAT!

Steph Curry proved this theory by becoming the best shooter in basketball and potentially in the history of the NBA.

Steph Curry was not the number one pick in his draft class. He was not even in the top five picks of the NBA draft that year. He was the *seventh* overall pick in the 2009 draft. People said he was too short, too slow, etc. This pissed Steph off, so he took CDA. He made a conscious decision to work on his shooting daily, so he could make a shot from anywhere on the court. Once he was able to do that, he raised his standards even higher. One example of this is the drill that Steph does to finish his practices. When he is exhausted, he goes to the free-throw line and shoots ten consecutive swooshes in the basket before he allows himself to go home. Just think about that for a second.

Most people would be happy making ten consecutive shots, even if they bounced in off the rim or off the backboard. Shaquille O'Neal is a hall of fame basketball player, but his lifetime free-throw percentage is only 52.7 percent. Shaq would probably do a backflip to get ten baskets in a row, let alone swooshes. For Steph, if the ball scrapes or nicks the rim and still goes in, then it does not count. He has to start all over from zero. This swoosh drill is one of the reasons he has become potentially the greatest basketball shooter in NBA history.

Steph's standard is not making a basket; it is making the perfect shot every time. He was not the most talented or best shooter when he was drafted. It was consistent daily action and raising his standards that allowed him to become great.

Now, my questions for you is: what standard do you hold yourself to? Are you holding yourself to a low standard or a perfect standard in your quest? If you raise your standard and stairstep your way to becoming great, you will be amazed at what you can achieve. Remember, it takes time and daily, consistent action. What areas of your life are you going to raise your standards in today? Only you know these things. When you are tougher on yourself and do not allow yourself to go to bed until you have reached your new standards, then things start to move in the right direction for you. It is amazing how these daily, consistent actions and the raising of your standards start to compound your results over time.

INDECISION STEALS HOURS AND YEARS FROM YOUR LIFE

I see a lot of people who are overwhelmed or sit in indecision. This is when people are idle and do not take action. Indecision steals hours and years from your life. Do not waste your most precious asset (time) thinking about what might go wrong. Instead, take the necessary actions to make your dreams a reality.

> *"Take the first step in faith. You don't have to see the whole staircase, just take the first step."*

—MARTIN LUTHER KING

In my opinion, the worst possible thing you can do is sit in indecision. This could cause you to go in a downward spiral of depression, anxiety, and so on.

There are many reasons why people feel it is OK to sit in indecision, but here are just a few examples:

- **Fear of change:** Change can be scary, but everything we want in life is just on the other side of fear. As much as we do not like it, one of the constants in life is change. Once we accept that everything is always evolving and changing, this fear will go away. Lao Tzu said, "A journey of a thousand miles begins with a single step."

- **Analysis paralysis:** Some of us feel we need to know everything about a subject before we get started. That is just an excuse. Logically, our brains know we will never know everything about a subject, because once we learn something new, there will always be more to learn.

- **Fear of not being good enough:** Many of us feel we have to be perfect at something before we start something new. Logically we will never do anything perfectly the first time. That is why I spoke earlier about giving yourself permission to suck and the story about the baby learning to walk. As humans, we do not react logically; we react emotionally. Even though we know this, our brains still play tricks on us. The more failures or learning experiences you have, the faster you will reach success. I tell people, "Done is better than perfect."

- **Fear of success:** A lot of us start to worry about things that may or may never happen. "Well, I cannot start a new business, Hugh, because if I do, then I will have to pay more tax in the future." If _____, then I will have to _____. This is our brain trying to keep us in the same place.

Any of these fears may cause your head to spin, and you may avoid taking the necessary actions to be successful. This is especially true when you are going against social norms to start a new business venture, invest in real estate, or do anything out of your comfort zone.

CHANGE THE STORY IN YOUR HEAD

I have a saying: "Dragons are real, but they are imaginary!" What this simply means is we create these stories in our heads about fear, problems, etc. We battle our own brain even when we know logically those fears or problems do not exist.

A perfect example of this is: have you ever prepared for an argument or a fight that never happened? Well, this was the dragon you were fighting in your head. You waste as much, if not more, time and brainpower thinking about the problem that might happen versus simply taking the action to prevent it. The fastest way out of your head is to take action!

"Get comfortable being uncomfortable."

—DAVID GOGGINS

Often, the first thing you need to change is your thoughts. Your brain wants to keep you in your comfort zone. However, to reach a better place emotionally, financially, spiritually, etc., you need to do things differently. When your brain gets uncomfortable, a simple trick you can tell yourself is, "I understand this might be scary, brain, but I am going to try something new today." This is one of the ways you can hack your brain. This will pacify your brain for a few minutes, hours, or until your old thought patterns return. You will have to continue repeating this until whatever you are doing becomes your new normal. Once it becomes your new normal, then you will notice how your wording will change. Watch how my wording even changed about running.

For over twenty years, I would say, "I cannot run more than three miles," or "I do not like to run, but I will play any sport that has a ball in it." My limiting beliefs and thoughts were holding me back from reaching my full running potential. I started training to run the Country Music Half-Marathon for charity with Team in Training after my mom was diagnosed with cancer. Somewhere along my daily training process with coaches and mentors to motivate me, my brain did a reassociation. I remember one day my mentor asked me, "How far did you run today?" and my response was, "I only ran three miles." I stopped in my tracks and started laughing out loud. Three miles is nothing for most runners, but for me, it had been a limiting belief. This reassociation did not happen overnight. It happened because of consistent daily training.

We can train our brains or bodies to be able to handle any situation. It just takes practice and time. That simple change in wording or reassociation in my brain was profound. I went on to run three half-marathons. What limiting beliefs are holding you back from reaching success or building your dream life?

WHY WON'T AN ADULT ELEPHANT RUN AWAY?

A more general example of a limiting belief is the reason why an adult elephant can be tied to a small pole in the ground and never run away. When elephants are young, they are tied to strong poles that are buried deep in the ground. The young elephant pulls and pulls and cannot move the pole or break free. Eventually, the elephant stops trying to move the pole. As an adult, the elephant never even tries to pull the pole out of the ground, because in its mind, the pole is an immovable object and it is a waste of time and energy. They just accept that this is their life, and they cannot break free.

The reality is it would only take a small amount of energy and effort from a large elephant to break free. Yet, it does not even try because it still believes the story in its head that it cannot move the pole. The elephant's thoughts have been conditioned, and it has placed a limiting belief in its life.

My question for you is, when did you become the adult elephant tied to the little pole holding you back from reaching your dreams?

Somewhere along your journey in life, you decided that you only deserve X. X is what you have settled for in your life financially, relationship-wise, spiritually, etc. You have created a limiting belief in your head that what you currently have is all you deserve. This is based on things from your past, choices you have made, or choices you did not make. You blame yourself for these failures, but these things keep you right where you are in life. Stop limiting yourself and change the story in your head.

What limiting belief(s) have you put on your life?

Congratulations for recognizing you have been holding yourself back from the life you deserve, but understand we place limiting beliefs on ourselves throughout life.

Let me give you another example. As you went through school, someone might have told you that you were either good or bad at math. If they told you that you were good at math, then you accepted that statement. This made learning math easier and faster. If they told you that you were bad at math, then you accepted that statement and put a limiting belief on yourself.

We do not like to do something we are not good at. This makes learning math harder and reinforces this limiting belief, but it is all just a story in your head. For those of you who feel you are bad at something, simply change your story to, "I am getting better at _____." Watch how your brain now allows you to learn and improve on that skillset.

We all have stories in our heads that are holding us back. I have watched this same thing play out with my team members, students, and in my own thoughts. Understand that phrases like, "I cannot," "I am not good at," and "I am bad at" are victim words. These are the little ropes that keep you tied to the pole, just like the elephant. They give your brain permission *not* to learn or improve that skill. I have gotten people to make huge changes in their success and abilities just by changing the words they use. I call it switching from victim words to leadership words. Let me give you an example.

NOT GOOD WITH TECHNOLOGY TO FIRST ONE ON CAMERA!

I have a team member whom I have worked with for over nine years. She had a story in her head about technology. She would say to everyone, "I am not good with technology." This was her excuse to not do something on a computer, Facebook, etc. Since she grew up before everyone had computers or cell phones, in her brain this was a valid excuse. How many people know someone who makes statements like that? They are 100 percent victim words!

Technology is a skill that can be learned; it just takes time and daily, consistent action. I recently got her to change the story in her head and do a reassociation each morning. She simply reads a message out loud that says, "I am learning to get better with technology." This statement gives her brain permission to learn and make mistakes. Since she did the reassociation, she has gotten 10,000 percent better with technology. In fact, when my team switched to a new webinar system, she was the first person to log in and figure out how to turn her web camera on. Now she is using Facebook and LinkedIn to grow her business, and she does online webinar trainings for my nationwide team. She has broken free from the rope and the pole by changing her victim words to leadership words.

What do you tell yourself that you are not good at? Change those victim words in your head to leadership words. Finish this statement: "I am learning and getting better at _____!" Once you change the words you use to leadership words and give your brain permission to learn and grow, you will be amazed at what you can learn to do. I dare you to try it. Write down the statement, tape it to your bathroom mirror, and read it out loud each morning.

ARE YOU LETTING EVERYONE ELSE CONTROL YOUR LIFE OR WILL YOU CONTROL YOUR LIFE?

A lot of people want to leave the corporate world because they want to be free and independent. They want to be able to build their own business their way. They might also rebel against sticking to a schedule. What they do not realize is that it is even *more* important to stick to a schedule when it comes to building your dream business and life. You will need to develop a scheduling discipline, or the universe will fill your schedule with things to distract you from reaching your goals and dreams. You do not realize how many actual minutes and hours you lose in your day from "Got a minute?" conversations, scrolling through social media, responding to random text messages, and "fake" emergencies in life and business. Studies say it takes eleven to twenty-five minutes to get back to concentrating on your initial task.

Do you feel like you have not gotten much done on building your goals and dreams at the end of the day? Well, that is why. There is an easy fix. It just takes building a new habit, a reassociation, holding the line, and protecting your schedule.

The general concepts are:

1. Either you set and control your schedule to build your business, or the universe will fill it with things to distract you from your goals.

2. You will subconsciously train people how to treat you and value your time. By making them schedule a meeting, they often will find the quick answers to their questions by themselves instead of waiting to meet with you. This is better for both of you in the long run.

3. You need to hold the line and protect your schedule (scheduling discipline).

This is the reassociation I have said over and over to my team, and a lot of them have used it to help them take control of their schedules. It goes like this: "By creating my daily schedule and protecting my time, I am making sure that I can achieve my goal/ dream to _____ and have the free and independent lifestyle that I want so I can _____."

Again, for this to be effective for you, you need to write it down on a piece of paper and tape it to your bedroom or bathroom mirror. Make sure to read it first thing in the morning and again at night before you go to bed. I know it sounds hokey, but it actually works. You picked up this book because you wanted to achieve something better in life. Now, you need to follow through and take the actions needed to support your goals and dreams.

Did you do it?

WANT MORE CONTROL IN LIFE?
HOLD THE LINE

We will always have lots of stuff going on in our lives, so that is not an excuse to let your schedule lapse. Now, remember the best part is *you* get to create your schedule and what works best for you and your body. There is no "standard" schedule. Once you create your schedule and put the important things into it, you will feel more in control of your life. The key now is to protect your schedule and hold the line.

As I was writing this chapter, I got a call from one of my students/ team members in Milwaukee, who just two weeks earlier had called because he was feeling down in the dumps. He did not feel like anything was going right in his life. He was not making the money that he wanted, and so forth. He was in a downward spiral, stuck in his head, and he felt the world was crashing in on him.

I told him, "The fastest way to get out of your head is to start taking action." He had already heard me say this over a hundred times in trainings and webinars. He was feeling frustrated because he was trying to manage his own marketing company and was no longer passionate about it, but it was paying his bills. He wanted to shift his focus to real estate investing and marketing businesses with a higher potential income. Plus, he wanted to open a restaurant, not to mention maintain his personal life. He was not being effective in *any* area of his life though, because he always felt behind. He felt like he was just spinning his wheels. Does this sound familiar?

"If you are serious, then you are going to create a schedule and dedicate a certain amount of time to each of the four things," I said. "You determine how much time to allocate to work on each one. However, once that amount of time is up, you stop, put down that business, and work on the next one."

When he called today, his first words were, "I feel more in control of my life since I implemented the schedule we talked about two weeks ago. Thank you!"

If you do not take control of your schedule and life, then the universe or other people will. The "Got a minute?" conversation or a fake emergency call or text are some of the biggest distractions to your time and energy. This is a rabbit hole that you want to avoid. Instead, it is all about training other people to respect your schedule and holding the line. You lose anywhere from ten minutes to three hours of your day each time you allow one of these things to disturb you. Not only do you lose time, but you also lose the momentum that you had working on a project or idea.

How do you hold the line without offending people? It is really very simple. You just text back, "Sorry, I am busy, but I do have time to help you at _____. Does that work for you?" If you have a calendar app and it is for business, then you just replace the last part with a link to your calendar app. I know people who tell others the next available slot in their calendar is in a week or two. If they respond with "Never mind," or just do not respond, then you know this was a "fake emergency." They have either figured it out themselves or were simply being lazy. If they book a meeting or accept your proposed time, then you know it is actually important. By holding the line on your schedule and doing this repeatedly, it will become easier for you. You will have more time to work towards your goals and dreams.

DEALING WITH NAYSAYERS

Unfortunately, most people have a lot of naysayers in their life (family, friends, and even themselves at times). Everyone wants to give you their opinion, especially when you are making a major life change. Do not listen to other people's opinions of you (or be influenced by them) if they are at your level of success in that area. This might sound harsh. However, you know it is true. If you listen to these people, you will never take action or achieve the life you deserve. You should only listen to people's opinions who have been where you want to be. They have already gone through the fire and come out on the other side stronger. They have achieved the success that you want to achieve. They can help prepare you for your own journey to success.

You might even feel pressure from your own mind because of past failures or learning experiences. Remember what Dr. Joe Dispenza says: "Your brain is a record of the past." When you do something new, it will cause you to be uncomfortable. You will need positive influences to help keep you moving forward.

How do I know you need this? Because I have to fight these same ANTs every time I do something new or start a new business. I need to be surrounded by positive influences as well.

I was in Toronto, Canada, attending a book-writing training and had spent the previous day working on this book. I had stayed up until 1:00 a.m. flushing out all of the chapters and outlining the key ideas for each chapter. That morning as I stood brushing my teeth in the bathroom, my past thoughts and fears started to attack me out of the blue. Thoughts like, *You can't spell. You do not know grammar, so how can you write a book? Your book is going to suck. What if the editors hate your idea?*

These ANTs and limiting beliefs came rushing into my mind and were so unexpected, they blindsided me. I could feel my thoughts going down a spiral, and I did not want to attend day two of the workshop. I had to turn off my electric toothbrush, look myself in the eye in the mirror, and say, "Shut up, brain and fears. I know what you are trying to do, and it isn't going to work." I finished brushing my teeth, got ready, and walked over to the training location. I showed my book, chapters, and concept to all three editors, and they really liked it. After each one made a few more minor tweaks, they all said, "I can't wait to read your book." Take that, brain and fears!

STOP LISTENING TO FRIENDS AND FAMILY

In my opinion, the worst thing you can do is listen to friends and family when it comes to launching a new business. Most of the time, they do not understand the amount of time you have put into researching your dream. They only see you for who you were and not who you are becoming.

Sometimes, friends and family question your ideas about changing careers because they feel they are protecting you. When I fired my boss, my dad was really concerned, because I was giving up my income, my corporate benefits, and health insurance. He pretty much called me stupid (in a nice way) and was totally against me leaving my corporate position. He knew I had no experience selling anything, let alone real estate education products. His fear was that I would not be able to make money and afford to live in NYC anymore. Plus, I was giving up my future in the IT industry, which he felt was very secure. I knew he did this out of love, and in his opinion he was trying to protect me from making a mistake. I had a strong "why" after 9/11 though, and I was not going to let him or anyone else dissuade me from building my dream life.

I know you have a strong why for wanting to make a big change as well. Remember the why that you created earlier in this book? Are you going to let a family member or friend stop you from building the life that you deserve?

Other naysayers do it because they want to keep you where you are in life. Often, it is because if you improve or change, then they will have to look at their life and decide if they need to change as well. Often, they do this out of fear.

When a naysayer approaches me, I play a game in my mind:

1. Are they where I want to be in life?

2. Do they have experience and are they successful in the area they are trying to counsel me in?

If the answer to either question is yes, then I am happy and willing to listen to their advice. If I do not know their background in the area, I simply ask them, "Can you tell me why you are an expert or have been successful in _____?"

If the answers are no to both, then I try to determine whether they are giving me their opinion out of concern, love, or fear.

- If it is out of concern or love, then I appreciate their concern and tell them that. I then explain the research and I reassure them I know what I am doing.

- Some people want to keep you where you are out of fear that you will pass them by or not need them, or they need to be right because of their ego, so I do not argue with them. You know these people, right? I simply say, "Thank you for your opinion."

Another question I get is, "Hugh, does it get easier? Do naysayers go away once you become successful?"

The answer is no. Life is like a mirror and will reflect your own thoughts back on you through people you know. The universe or whatever you believe in will continue to test you to see if you are serious about making a change in your life or following through with your goals and dreams. Especially when you are doing something scary for you. You just get better at not hearing them and avoiding the roadblocks.

I flew back from that book-writing training in Toronto to celebrate my mom's birthday. My brother asked me, "What were you doing in Toronto?"

"I went there for a conference on how to write a book," I said.

His first words were, "You are scaring me! You cannot spell or understand grammar. How can you write a book?"

I love my brother to death. He was just verbalizing my own thoughts and fears, and the universe was testing me to see if I was serious about writing this book. Not everyone will be in your corner or offer support. That is their problem and not yours. His statement fueled me to complete this book and start the eFramily Ohana community.

Do You Need More Positive People and Support?

Bonus: I have had a goal to build an "Entrepreneur Framily" or eFramily that can support entrepreneurs in all aspects of their life. As entrepreneurs, we are all a little messed up, and that is what makes us great. We are wonderful and strong in certain areas of our lives. However, there are a few areas where we are weak or a hot mess. I have found wonderful support groups for specific areas of life like men's groups and business groups. I have not found a community that fully supports all areas of life, or one that supports relationships, business, personal finance, lifestyle, and charities. That is why I created the eFramily Ohana community to provide this holistic support.

"Ohana" is a Hawaiian word that refers to your extended family. This is not just your family but also the friends and community who support you. As part of the "eFramily Ohana," you will have support in every area of your life to help you become the best version of you. I will continue to have your back and give you support as long as you are willing to do the work and keep moving forward. To learn more, go to eFramily.com.

In addition to the naysayer exercise above, here are some ideas that you can use to help you stay positive and surround yourself with the right support:

1. Find some positive podcasts, YouTube channels, or Audible books that you can listen to and build a stronger mindset.

2. Seek out positive, successful people who you want to surround yourself with and learn from.

3. Remember, when you get down to that "The easiest thing to do in life is to quit. So, why quit now?" Just take one more step, one more action, one more _____ and see what happens.

4. If you want more positive support, go to eFramily.com and join our eFramily Ohana and create a free account. You can also join our free private Facebook group at

eFramily.com or facebook.com/groups/eframily. Here you will find many like-minded individuals who will support you on your journey.

THE STORY OF THE BAMBOO

The unfortunate thing is that most people do not give their ideas, dreams, etc. enough time to grow. They want success immediately, and it does not happen that way. World-class is a process. Think about how bamboo grows. We all know that bamboo grows quickly and spreads fast. What a lot of people do not know is that it can take five years for bamboo to grow enough to poke out of the ground. Just think about that for a second. A farmer has to plant the bamboo seed and then provide good soil, water, and sunshine for five years before they will see any results for their hard work.

Just think of what could happen on any given day during those five years. If the farmer decides not to water the spot where he planted it, or a neighbor/family member comes over and says, "You have been watering that same spot for years now and have had no results. Wouldn't the smart thing to do be to stop wasting your time and plant something else instead?" What if the farmer does not water the spot two, three, or even seven days in a row, or gets freaked out about the cost of watering with no income for five years? That bamboo would never grow! The first five years is a test of the farmer's will, patience, and belief.

The first five years will be a test of your will, patience, and belief in your new idea, business, passion, etc. You will need to learn new skills, be able to handle the emotional and financial roller coaster, and deal with the naysayers in your life. If you continue to take daily consistent action toward your goals and dreams, you will eventually see the fruit of your labor just as the farmer did.

"Don't judge each day by the harvest that you reap but by the seeds that you plant."

—ROBERT LOUIS STEVENSON

Once the bamboo sprouts out of the dirt, it doubles in size each and every year. You will find the same thing happens in your business as you master your emotions and the skills you need to learn. Your business should also double and triple in size until you need to learn the next skill or lesson. Give yourself permission and time to grow your business. Remember, the famous photographer Henri Cartier-Bresson said, "Your first 10,000 photographs are your worst."

Keep the faith and your consistent, daily actions. Then watch your business sprout and double in size.

ARE YOU WILLING TO GIVE YOURSELF ENOUGH TIME TO BE SUCCESSFUL?

Most people, when they start a new business, never give themselves enough time to learn and develop the skills necessary to blossom into a successful entrepreneur or real estate investor.

You need to give yourself permission to suck and grow through your mistakes until you become unconsciously competent in your business. Remember, CDA leads to success. If you give yourself time to allow this to happen, your entrepreneurial business and/or real estate investing will take off at such an extreme speed, you will generate so much income that all you can do is try to keep pace.

I believe there are four levels of learning:

1. **Unconscious incompetent:** Things you do not know that you do not know. I already told you, I did not know there was a speaking and training industry that taught real estate investing. I did not even know to ask about it.

2. **Conscious incompetent:** Things you know that you do not know. I know that I do not know how to fix a car's engine. I could learn, but I do not want to.

3. **Conscious competent:** Things you know but have to think about to answer. It could be a recipe you used to make, or it could be a story from your past, etc.

4. **Unconscious competent:** Things you know and do not even have to think about. Like taking a shower, brushing your teeth, or your drive to work or home. You just go on autopilot and do it.

A great example of how we go from unconscious incompetent to unconscious competent is learning to tie your shoelaces. As a baby, you did not know how to tie your shoelaces, and you did not care. You were unconscious incompetent. As you got a little older, you would watch your parents or siblings tie your shoelaces for you, and you became conscious incompetent. Eventually, you learned how to tie your shoelaces, but had to think about it, making you conscious competent. Now, you are unconscious competent in tying your shoelaces. You do not even think about it. Heck, you can be talking on the phone, chewing gum, and tying your shoelaces at the same time, because it does not take any energy or brainpower. When you are unconscious competent in your business, health, real estate, etc., you will see exponential growth and riches come in faster than you can believe. You just have to go through the different stages, and it takes time to master these skills.

Say No to Things that Do Not Serve Your Passion and Purpose

One of the hardest things in life for most people to do is to say no to things that will not help them achieve their goals. People are afraid of hurting relationships or are validated by serving other people. These people tend to be the ones who overcommit to things not related to their goals and then do not feel like they get anything accomplished.

> *"The difference between successful people and really successful people is that really successful people say no to almost everything."*

—WARREN BUFFETT

There are probably a lot of things in your life that are taking up your time and are not helping you reach your goal or dream. These things all zap your energy and suck up your time.

I watch people show up every week all across the US to serve a community of entrepreneurs and real estate investors. These same people could be generating $1,000 to $11,000-plus a week at the same events if they simply took a couple of hours each week to do moneymaking activities. Instead, they let other things get in their way and avoid the moneymaking activities necessary to get paid. They think they are building their business, but the reality is they are just volunteering their time.

They are telling themselves a lie that "being busy" equals building a business. To be clear, everyone is busy. You are either busy working toward your goals or moving further away from them.

Get Crystal Clear and Specific about Your Goals

The first step is to get crystal clear on your goals. This way when someone approaches you with a business idea, opportunity, etc., you can pull out your goal sheet and see if what they are asking you is in line with your goals or not. If not, you say, "Thank you, but I have a full plate of things to do. Maybe in the future we can talk about ___ again." You then add it to your list of things to do in the future. This only works when you are clear on your goals and what you want to achieve.

You are actually doing yourself and the other person a favor. Being up front and honest with them prevents hurt feelings or even regrets about wasting each other's time. You can stop this by using your goals/passion as the guide to ensure you are being productive with your time.

EXERCISE:
Identify and Break Limiting Beliefs

Do you want your answers in a digital format? If so, go to thelaunchbuttonbook.com and click the login button to create your own The Launch Button Blueprint for Success PDF!

I want you to watch your own energy, emotions, and breathing when you say these words out loud. Stand in front of a mirror and say the next three phrases:

- "I am overwhelmed with my finances."

- "I am stressed out because I have so many things to do."

- "I do not know what to do with my life."

What did you notice about your shoulders, your breathing, and your energy? Most people see their shoulders slump and get small. They also notice they feel down or have less energy.

Now, I want you to watch in the mirror your own energy, emotions, and breathing when you say out loud:

- "I have lots of opportunities to make money."

- "I have so many opportunities to grow and improve."

- "I have the power to create and design my life the way I want it to be moving forward."

How do you feel now? Most feel excited and have hope. They also feel their shoulders go back and they feel taller. You can see the power of the words that we use. Sometimes, we do not realize that we are taking away all of our own power by choosing our words poorly.

- **Which victim words do you use?** Write these out on a piece of paper.

OLD *VICTIM* WORDS		NEW *LEADERSHIP* WORDS
Example: I am feeling overwhelmed	→	Example: I have lots of opportunities
I am not good at: _____ _____	→	I am learning to get better at: _____ _____

- **Who are the naysayers and people who cause you stress that you may need to remove or limit in your life?**

- **What activities are you doing that are not in line with your goals and dreams?** Write down the three to five activities that you are doing weekly that are not in line with your goals. How much time are you spending weekly on each activity? How much time would you get back in your day or week to build your business? Now, you have the choice to completely eliminate these activities or make them a reward when you achieve a goal or reach a mile-stone in your life or new business.

- **What reassociations do you have to make to reach your next goal?** I have gotten people to make huge changes in their success and/or abilities just by changing the words they use. Write out your new goals or desired outcome with leadership words.

5

Real Estate Investing and Entrepreneurship Go Hand in Hand

The uber-successful entrepreneurs have always had a real estate component in their portfolio. Multiple streams of income give you a backup plan and protection for your business during downturns in the economy.

THE AMERICAN REVOLUTION WAS FOUGHT BY ENTREPRENEURS and landowners against the tyranny of the British rule. Being an entrepreneur is in every American's DNA, and our constitution was written by them. Over generations and through traditional schooling, we have been made to choose careers based on our fears and our need for job security. Most people think going to school and getting a good job will lead to financial security. It is only after they become frustrated at their job, encounter other roadblocks, or have a trauma in their life that they consider starting their own business. The skills required to start and build a successful business are not taught in most traditional schools or even business schools. Isn't that crazy?

Just about every wealthy person on the *Forbes* 400 list for 2020 is a business owner and real estate investor. This formula has been proven through the test of time. It goes all the way back to the Rockefellers and the Vanderbilts. Remember, as I mentioned earlier McDonald's owns some of the most expensive corners in all of the world.

You may in fact need multiple businesses, real estate projects, or income streams to protect you from the next Black Swan event. I personally like having six to eight different income streams from businesses, side hustles, and real estate investments. This way, if I lose one or two, then I still have four to six other ways of generating income.

TAKING PERSONAL RESPONSIBILITY AND HAVING THE DISCIPLINE TO REACH YOUR GOALS

Discipline in our society is a *bad* word. However, you do need to discipline your mind, body, spending habits, etc. if you want to achieve your goals and dreams. It does not mean you do not get to have fun, travel, or enjoy life. It just means you get to do these things once you achieve certain goals or benchmarks. Discipline prevents you from sacrificing long-term wealth for a short-term dopamine rush that you will regret later.

You are a grown adult, and as such, I will expect you to take personal responsibility for your actions and have the discipline to create new habits to reach your goals. Now is the time for you to declare that you are going to create discipline in all of the areas of your life, including financial responsibility. *Only* if you build discipline and truly want to become financially free will I share the financial secrets of the wealthy.

If you cannot declare to yourself, your significant other, and everyone in your life that you are going to create discipline and take full responsibility, then **stop here** and go back and review the first four chapters of this book to change your mindset. If you *do not* fully commit to building discipline and taking responsibility, then this next section can get you into trouble.

Are you ready?

THERE IS TREMENDOUS POWER IN OWNING AND RUNNING A BUSINESS

Congratulations on your commitment to building discipline in all areas of your life. The plan I am going to lay out for you over the next few sections will require you to continue to build discipline and new habits. It will challenge a lot of your previous financial mindsets and may even freak you out at times. You could potentially become your own bank, learn to pay for debt with debt, and many other wealth-building concepts. These techniques may seem strange at first, but they work. I will cover these topics and more later in this book. That is why it is important to continue to learn as you go through life. There is so much information on the internet. However, they always leave out crucial information on the free online trainings. This is why you want to surround yourself with top-notch people in their field or industry.

One of the hardest things to do as an entrepreneur is to find people who think like you and have the same goals. You need to search and find these people or join groups that support entrepreneurs like the eFramily community.

I 100 percent believe, like the founders of our country—George Washington, Thomas Jefferson, etc.—that every American should own their own small business. I do not care if you sell lemonade on the street corner or you follow the steps in this book to launch your dream business and become a real estate investor. There are lots of tax benefits and other benefits of owning a small business.

A major advantage of owning a business is that you control your income. As an employee of a company, you usually have very little control of your income, time off, and schedule. The very first thing that comes out of your paycheck is taxes. Most people lose 30–35 percent of their income before they even see any money. Plus, as an employee taxpayer, you only get ten to twenty tax deductions based on the income that you make. In America, we have some of the worst work–life balances in the world. Most people start off with only two weeks PTO and it takes years to build up to four weeks. Remember they also control your schedule with the 50x40x40 trap we talked about back in Chapter One.

With a business, it is the exact opposite. You generate income, have expenses from your business, and if there is anything left over at the end, then you pay tax on your profits. This is exactly what large companies do. If you use the right tax strategies, you can turn some or all of your travel into a business tax deduction. You can have unlimited PTO as long as it is related to your business activities. (Check with your CPA first.) Plus, you now control your schedule and can create your own hours. However, most Americans are too afraid to take advantage of all the tax deductions that are available to a business owner. Did you know there are over three hundred tax deductions for a business?

WHY DO YOU WANT TO OWN A SMALL BUSINESS?

Talking about expenses, you can potentially legally turn a lot of your regular day-to-day expenses into expenses for your new business. I am not a CPA or an attorney, so you will need to work with them to qualify your expenses. I have worked with a lot of CPAs and attorneys, and here are some of the more common business tax deductions that you can potentially take for your business:

- Travel: as long as more than 50 percent of your trip is business-related

- Meals/Food: you have to eat on these trips, right?

- Technology: cell phone, computer, Apple watch, etc.

- Funding of retirement accounts

- Health insurance

- Hiring your kids under age eighteen

- And many more

It is very important that you track your expenses to document your tax deductions for your accountant or CPA. Per the disclosure above, you will want to work with a competent CPA to go over your personal situation before taking these tax deductions. I just wanted to activate your brain's RAS to the potential tax deductions that could be written off each year by starting a business.

ASSET PROTECTION AND LEGACY PLANNING

A business will also help you set up your asset protection. If done properly, it can help you set up legacy planning for your family for generations to come. How would you like to be the next Rockefeller of your family? Now you will work with a competent CPA and/or attorney to set up your asset protection and legacy planning. Having structured a business or businesses the right way can protect you and your family in a lawsuit and will allow you to pass on the benefits to future generations.

These benefits can be anything from ownership in a business, real estate, dividends, or other passive income. This can preserve your legacy and future generations just as the Rockefeller family did.

These asset protection vehicles include:

- Health insurance

- Will and testament

- Life insurance

- 401(k)s, SEP, IRAs, etc.

- Insurance for your business, properties, real estate, etc.

- Trusts

There are many more benefits to owning a business, but it also is a vehicle that allows you to build cash flow to give you the time and freedom to travel the world and do what you want, when you want. You can also set up overfunded life insurance policies to become your own bank in the future to fund businesses, college tuition, and homes for yourself, your children, or grandkids. It is not going to be easy in the beginning, but if you are willing to put the time into it, then it will be something that you can be proud of and pass on to future generations.

THE POWER OF REAL ESTATE INVESTING

There is one more powerful benefit to owning a business. When you combine the power of a business with real estate investing, you can become unstoppable. More millionaires have been made by investing in real estate than in any other profession over the history of time. There are three main reasons why governments fight wars: religion, resources, and politics. The underlying reason is almost always to acquire land. If you look back through the history of time, the people who controlled the land controlled the wealth.

Investing and Entrepreneurship Go Hand in Hand

Real estate has many benefits, including providing one of the three basic needs of every human being. Every human needs food, water, and shelter. Real estate is your shelter from the elements, and everyone needs a home or shelter to protect them. Most people appreciate you wearing clothing in public. However, there are people who run around naked on islands and survive. Heck, they have even created a reality survival TV show about it. This is why real estate will never go out of style.

Our population continues to grow, so the style of the shelter may change over time from caves and huts to houses and buildings, but it is still real estate. One of the things that I love about real estate investing is that it will never go to zero. Yes, the real estate market will crash just like Bitcoin, cryptocurrency, the stock market, gold, silver, etc. That is just the cycle of a market. That is why I train my students to go into each one of their real estate deals with three exit strategies that will protect them from an unforeseen crash or Black Swan event. No one can predict a crash. People take educated guesses. However, if you have a plan before you buy your real estate, then in case of a crash, you can protect yourself.

The Myth: You Need Good Credit, a Job, and Verifiable Income to Buy Real Estate

The government, banks, etc. all want you to own real estate. Unfortunately, a significant amount of the population does not feel that they can own their own homes or invest in real estate. The average American only knows three ways to invest in real estate:

1. **Traditional Way:** Most people feel they need a good job, credit, and verifiable income plus a down payment to qualify for a traditional mortgage.

2. **Cash, Other People's Money (OPM) or Hard Money Loan (HML):** You either save all of the money or borrow from a family member or friend (OPM) to pay all cash for the property. In this case, your credit score does not matter. If you cannot borrow all of the money, then there are hard money lenders and/or private lenders who will lend you money at a higher

interest rate. Your credit does not matter as much and they are more flexible to do short-term loans.

3. **Trying to Learn Wholesaling on "YouTube University":** Wholesaling does not require money or credit, but it does take *a lot* of time. Unfortunately, most YouTubers leave out critical information. Some states are changing their laws to make wholesaling without a real estate license illegal. This is something that you will need to pay attention to and research.

Note: In my opinion, you should not do co-wholesaling. This is a strategy that is going around on the internet. I have watched a bunch of my students lose time, energy, and money on the deals that they found. This is because you are not protected by the Closing Disclosure form or a purchase and sale contract. The Closing Disclosure form is a legal document that shows who gets paid which amounts at the closing table. Since your name does not appear on the Closing Disclosure form or contract, it is up to the kindness of the other wholesaler to pay you your fee.

Breaking the Myth: No Matter Your Financial Situation, You Can Buy Real Estate

I do not care if you have $500 in a bank account and a 350 credit score, or you are a multimillionaire with an 800-plus credit score. Everyone can acquire real estate. There are over twenty strategies to acquire real estate. Now, some strategies require money and credit, and some do not. Let's be clear: it is way easier to buy real estate if you have good credit, a job, and verifiable income. Anything you can do to fix your own personal financial situation will, of course, make it easier and faster for you to invest in real estate. The strategies that do not require money or credit will take more time, energy, and effort to learn and master. You will need additional knowledge on ways to implement those strategies.

The most common strategies that people understand are fix and flip, buy and hold, and wholesaling. There are twenty-one-plus strategies and government programs that can help you acquire properties or buy your own home:

1. Pre-foreclosures

2. Foreclosures

3. Short sales

4. Real estate owned (REO)

5. Department of Housing and Urban Development (HUD)

6. Probate

7. Estate

8. Creative acquisitions

9. Subject-to

10. Veterans Affairs/Government

11. Bankruptcy

12. Multifamily

13. Commercial

14. Tax deed/lien

15. Lease option

16. Wholesaling

17. Auctions

18. Short-term rentals

19. Assisted living

20. Opportunity zones

21. Fix and flip

And many more.

One of these real estate investment strategies listed above is the right one for your current financial situation. It will allow you to acquire your own home or a rental property no matter the size of your bank account or your credit score. You must change the story in your head to: "I can learn to master _____ strategy that matches my financial situation to buy _____." I have helped students in every financial situation invest in real estate using this technique.

You will also have to master new skills, like how to talk to homeowners, negotiate the deal, etc. Remember, you will need to give yourself permission to suck as you go through the four levels of learning until you are able to master these skills.

If you have good credit, good income, and good savings, you will also want to learn these strategies because the banks will eventually stop lending to you. They will cap you out because your debt-to-income ratios will be too high. It helps if you can apply the above creative strategies along your real estate journey when needed.

I will go into detail about some of these strategies later in this book. I just wanted to start activating your RAS and open your mind to these possibilities.

CASH-FLOWING REAL ESTATE IS A NATURAL PROTECTION AGAINST A DOWNTURN IN YOUR BUSINESS

I believe in all twenty-plus strategies of real estate investing because between my own deals and coaching students through their deals, I have seen them all work. Real estate investing diversifies your income. Cash-flowing real estate properties are any properties that produce more income than the expenses of owning and maintaining said properties. This includes real estate taxes and debt services or mortgage payments. Cash-flowing real estate properties are a natural protection for a real estate market crash and/or a crash in your business or job.

We all understand every market has a cycle, and we are not psychic and cannot predict the future. Otherwise, we would all win the PowerBall. There are a few things you can do to protect yourself from a market downturn in your entrepreneur and real estate businesses.

First, understand every market will eventually crash—the stock market, Bitcoin, cryptocurrency, real estate, etc. This was the problem that most people did not consider or look at going into the crash of 2008. They just thought the market would continue to climb, and they did not have a backup exit plan in case the market crashed.

Second, understand a real estate market crash is like a bad haircut. A bad haircut typically takes two to six weeks to grow out. A market crash can last two to six years.

An easy way to explain a market cycle is to compare it to the four seasons (winter, spring, summer, and fall). The difference is that in a market cycle, a season can last for years or only a couple of months. You just have to recognize the signs of the market and which seasons your market cycle is in. The best time to buy properties is in the winter or when you are just moving into the spring. During the spring and summer, I have made good money fixing and flipping properties. Here you can generate large chunks of capital. During these times, money is plentiful, and you can get funding for your business and your deals. You still want to make sure that you go into each deal with three exit strategies in case the market changes in the middle of your flip.

In the fall of a market cycle, you want to shift into cash-flowing properties, because this is where long-term wealth is built.

What I like about cash-flowing properties is that even if your property value drops by 50 percent, you still maintain your cash flow. Let's say your cash flow is $400 a month on a single-family home after all expenses, and the value drops 50 percent in winter. Even though your property value dropped, it usually does not change the rent payment amount owed to you. You still receive your positive monthly cash flow of $400 a month.

You can technically afford to hold that property forever or until the market corrects itself. You will continue to receive the tax deductions of owning a property, and the benefit of your tenant paying your monthly mortgage payments, all the while building your cash reserves. If you have a traditional amortized mortgage, then you are getting wealthier each month. Every amortized loan payment is principle plus interest. This means your tenant is paying down the principle on your mortgage for you, and you are building equity in your property. When the market does recover, even if you sell it at the same price you bought it for, you will be able to cash out your newfound equity that your tenant paid for. This is 100 percent profit for you!

Note: The only Black Swan event that this was not true for was during the COVID-19 pandemic. To offset evictions due to major layoffs and unemployment, tenants were allotted temporary relief from paying their rent. However, the government is supposed to reimburse landlords or provide income to tenants to pay for back rent. Thus, payments have not ceased completely, they are just delayed.

This extra cash flow from your properties can help offset any crash in your entrepreneur income or job loss during a downturn. This will allow you to continue to support yourself, your family, and your current lifestyle. Properties do not go to zero like a stock or bond can. That is why I feel you need to have both.

TAX SAVINGS

Real estate investing also offers many different tax advantages to real estate investors—everything from tax deductions to tax credits. We have already outlined some of the potential tax deductions of owning a business earlier in this chapter. As a real estate investor, you get even more tax deductions and even tax credits.

Tax deductions are great, but tax credits are even better. What is the difference, you ask?

- **Tax deductions:** Reduce your taxable income by a percentage based upon your tax bracket. This means if a business has a $5,000 tax deduction and the business is in a 20 percent tax bracket, then the deduction is really worth only $1,000.

- **Tax credits:** This is a dollar-for-dollar reduction in your actual taxes owed. This means if you had a $5,000 business credit, then you get to deduct the full $5,000.

Some examples of tax deductions and tax credits are:

- **Depreciation:** The value that an asset like a house, car, computer, etc. will decrease over time due to use, wear and tear, or obsolescence. The example below is what you can do for a real estate asset. You can divide the value you bought the real estate for by the number of years below to get the amount you can depreciate each year on your taxes.

* Residential: 27.5 years

* Commercial: 39.5 years

Note: There is a debate on whether you want to take depreciation or not each year on your real estate assets, so talk with your CPA.

- **Cost segregation:** There are different assets that you need for your real estate investments and for running your business. These assets have different amortization schedules. They range anywhere from five years to twenty years. You will need a specialist to get the full cost segregation tax deductions. The average CPA does not know all of the deductions.

- **Write-off mortgage interest:** You can deduct the interest you pay on your primary mortgage on your taxes based on your income. You also can write off your **Home Equity Line of Credit** (HELOC) interest if it was used for home purchases or renovations. We will talk about how to pay off your mortgage faster by using a strategy to pay it off in up to one-third of the time later in this book.

- **Small business healthcare tax insurance:** You can get a tax credit of up to 50 percent of the health insurance premiums that you pay for your employees. You do not get the tax credit for any owner's health insurance premiums.

- **Going green in your business:** There are many different green tax credits that you can research. Two examples are purchasing an electric car and switching to green energy.

- **Real estate taxes:** You can deduct the amount you pay in real estate taxes up to $10,000.

Again, I am not a CPA or an attorney, and tax laws change each year. So, you will need to double-check with your local CPA and/or attorney.

Your entrepreneur business can provide the income to buy properties at their cheapest values during a crash and take advantage of the market conditions.

As mentioned earlier, the best time to buy properties and accumulate wealth is actually in winter or a downturn of the market. If your entrepreneur business continues to thrive in a real estate downturn, then this is the best time to buy more cash-flowing properties. Other investors or homeowners have to sell their properties on the cheap to save their credit or to avoid other financial problems. What most people do not realize is that during the real estate crash of 2008–2010 more millionaires were made by investing in real estate than in the twenty years before the crash!

Now, do you understand how your entrepreneur business and your cash-flowing real estate properties can offset each other during a crash?

EXERCISE:
Start Building Your Dream Team

Do you want your answers in a digital format? If so, go to thelaunchbuttonbook.com and click the login button to create your own The Launch Button Blueprint for Success PDF!

- Which roles or positions do you need on your team?

    * First, we need to identify the roles that are essential to your team. Here are some examples: accountants, attorneys, lenders/bankers, contractors, mentors/coaches, consultants, marketers, sales team, real estate title company, appraisers, property managers, cohosts (STR), Realtors, etc.

    * Once you have identified these roles, you can select someone you know for each role or put to be determined (TBD). You can get referrals from the people you have picked, or you can do some research for each position.

- **Who do you want on your dream team?** Remember, you do not have to settle and you do not have to accept things as they are. As your business grows, you may outgrow your team's knowledge or level of expertise. Let's dream and get advice from some of the best in your industry. Go back over your list and put your dream person for each position.

- **What questions should you ask your team members to make sure their expertise lines up with your goals or business idea?** There are different types of attorneys that I will use for general business knowledge versus real estate knowledge. I want you to determine a few questions to ask each one of your team members to get a better understanding of their level of knowledge or expertise.

  * For example, with real estate agents or Realtors, I always ask them what a 1030-something exchange is. It is actually called a "1031 Exchange." I accept two answers: the correct one, and "I do not know, but let me do some research and get back to you."

- Write down which real estate strategy (or strategies) you want to get started with. (Remember the twenty-one strategies from earlier in the chapter.)

6

How the Shared Economy Has Changed the World

The Shared Economy

The new shared economy is a disruptor and has opened up thousands of ways for people to generate income while following their passions.

A NEW "SHARED" OR "COLLABORATION" ECONOMY HAS emerged since the 2008 Black Swan event. You may have heard of it but may not know exactly what it is. Let's define it for you.

A **shared economy** is an economic model in which individuals are able to borrow or rent assets owned by someone else. The shared economy model is most likely to be used when the price of a particular asset is high, and the asset is not fully utilized all of the time.

Some examples are coworking spaces; talent sharing; ridesharing; car, bike, and scooter sharing; and of course, travel or real estate rentals/ownership. This is disrupting everything from taxis to hotels. More and more people are joining this economy in unique ways.

Remember, previously we discussed the picture of wealth based on when you were born. Here is how Bernard Marr (2006) describes the difference between the two in his *Forbes* article:

> *"Whereas being a 'two-car family' (or even three or four cars) was once a mark of status, today many millennials see more status in being a one-car or even zero-car family and making use of services like Uber, Lyft, CarGo, and others to use cars only when they need one."*

What does this mean for you? It means that we need to shift the way we think about investing in real estate and building businesses. The shared economy is constantly disrupting industries. If you were born before 1983, then you need to stop thinking like it is 1920. So stop and learn how to harness the power of the new shared economy. You will also need to make a few tweaks to your current financial situation. I believe the lifestyle of your dreams is achievable or something pretty darn close to it. You just need to learn how to use and maximize the *new* shared economy.

One of the biggest and simplest things to do is to turn your home (which technically is a liability) into an asset and then duplicate the process in all of your dream vacation destinations. Your dream can be as simple as having one vacation property all the way to having twenty properties in different countries. What if you could spend two weeks to two months a year in each of your dream vacation locations and generate enough money to support the lifestyle that you want?

I do not know if it was just my upbringing and watching my parents struggle financially that influenced me, but I have always looked for angles or ways to monetize my life. Now I get paid to do the things I would just do normally. There are all different ways that you can generate value or income for people and turn things that you normally pay for into ways of generating money. Even though I was born before 1983, I have been using this shared economy model and math for most of my life. I have been paid to travel, speak, drink, have fun, and even run. With my students, I have come up with lots of creative ways to have fun and get paid.

I will give you more ideas in later chapters but for now, I want to focus on bigger assets. The shared economy allows people to get their cars, homes, vacation properties, boats, planes, etc. paid for by other people. Are you ready to learn how to do this?

IF IT IS GOOD ENOUGH FOR WARREN BUFFETT...

The first time I heard about the shared economy was when Warren Buffett made a huge investment in NetJets. NetJets is a company that provides shared airplanes. We all know flying is expensive, especially if you do it privately. Owning a plane for your company or yourself is very expensive, plus there are fees and maintenance. NetJets sells shares in an airplane. You could then fly privately without having to pay for maintenance, the pilots, or any other headaches that come with owning an airplane.

DISRUPTING THE TAXI INDUSTRY

Uber, Lyft, Via, and other companies have been huge disruptors to the taxi industry. These ridesharing apps allow anyone with a car that qualifies to pick up and drop off passengers anywhere. It has provided an excellent source of secondary income for people. Uber likes to call it your "side hustle," but it can also supplement your income.

As much as the cities want to fight these apps, they are well used by people. Most major cities have always had some form of taxi service, and they limited the number of licensed taxis by controlling the sale of taxi medallions or a license. The price of New York City's yellow taxi medallion increased to over $1,000,000 in 2013. Banks and private lenders funded the purchases of taxi medallions because it was a very lucrative business.

The disruption by rideshare companies has caused the price of an NYC taxi medallion to drop below $500,000. According to *Curbed New York*, in 2019, 950 NYC taxi medallion holders had to file bankruptcy (Ricciulli 2019). This scenario unfortunately is being repeated all around the globe for taxi drivers.

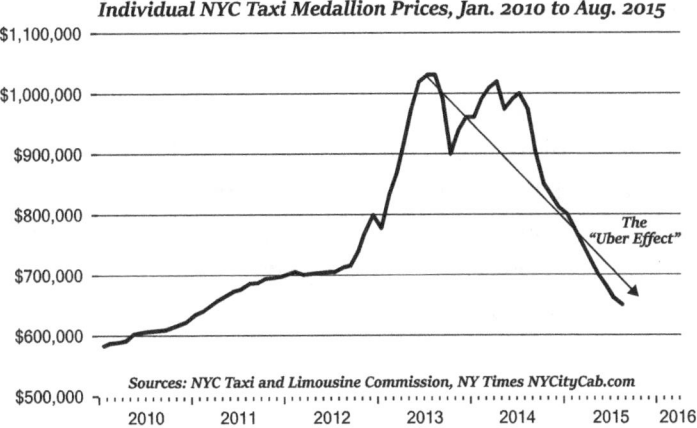

Sources: NYC Taxi and Limousine Commission, NY Times NYCityCab.com

"The 'Uber Effect'" 2015.

WANT SOMEONE ELSE TO PAY FOR
YOUR DREAM CAR?

Enter "Tauro," where you can actually rent out your own car while you travel, sleep, or for just a few days a month. You do not just have to do this with your current car; you could actually lease or buy your dream car and then calculate how many days you would need to rent it out to cover your monthly expenses. Who knows where this will lead? Tesla is testing a way to let your car drive around and pick people up while you sleep. A few of the rental car companies are changing their business models to keep up with the new shared economy.

WHAT ABOUT HOTELS AND TRAVEL?

According to *Newsweek*, in 2018, global tourism increased to 1.4 billion international arrivals per year (Avery 2019). International travel has slowed down due to COVID. Just like after 9/11, it will take some time for people to be comfortable traveling internationally, on an airplane, or on a cruise ship. However, there has not been a slowdown in people wanting to travel and experience places like a local.

THE WORLD'S TOP TRAVELING NATIONS

This shows the world's top ten traveling nations, their tourism expenditure, and their air miles per person.

	Country Rank	Tourism Expenditure	Air Miles Per Person
01	China	$257.7 Billion	65 Air Miles
02	United States	$135 Billion	227 Air Miles
03	Germany	$89.1 Billion	285 Air Miles
04	United Kingdom	$71.4 Billion	271 Air Miles
05	France	$41.4 Billion	80 Air Miles
06	Canada	$31.8 Billion	632 Air Miles
07	Korea	$30.6 Billion	195 Air Miles
08	Italy	$27.7 Billion	130 Air Miles
09	Australia	$34.2 Billion	573 Air Miles
10	Russia	$31.1 Billion	87 Air Miles

Roser 2017.

DO YOU KNOW HOW AIRBNB GOT STARTED?

Some apartment and house-sharing apps got their start from couch surfing. Yes, you read that right. You can still stay on a stranger's couch as you travel from city to city for free. Now VRBO has been around for a while in more traditional rental vacation spots. However, Airbnb took short-term rentals to a whole different level. Most people do not know the Airbnb origin story. Do you know how they got started?

They started by renting out air mattresses in a garage for music festivals and conventions. Hence, the name, Airbnb. From there, they grew to shared spaces, full places, and now million-dollar-plus homes. They are the 800-pound gorilla in the short-term rental business. Sometimes we say, "Did you book an Airbnb?" and we mean, "Did you book a short-term rental?"

Because of this disruption, some larger cities are changing their laws because they are struggling with how short-term rentals and the hotel industry can coexist. Other locations are seeing an explosion in short-term rentals as people want more space outside of cities. Some cities and states have fully embraced this model.

Note: It will be your responsibility to stay informed as the laws and regulations continue to change and the short-term rental business continues to also grow and change.

To get the latest information, plug into the eFramily community or watch my weekly update on social media.

DO YOU WANT TO BE PART OF THE $38 BILLION INDUSTRY?

People today want to travel globally and yet stay like a local. What if you could leverage the real estate investment strategies that we touched on earlier to acquire properties in your dream locations? You could then rent them out using this shared economy model. You can have the best of both worlds. This is an opportunity that you have today! Are you excited now? Are you ready to push the launch button and make this happen?

You might be saying to yourself, *I am excited, but I am not sure my idea for a business is going to work.* Well, if your idea is to create some sort of experience for people, then I might have the solution for you. You can test it and get paid without a lot of capital expense up front.

Creating Experiences *and* Getting Paid to Test Your Idea?

You do not need to own or control a property to make money on Airbnb right now. You can create an experience for locals or people traveling to the area. If you want to create something more technical or in another industry, then you can find a different site that will allow you to do the same thing for your audience. These experiences can be anything that you want them to be—cooking lessons, guided hikes, workouts, food tours, bar crawls, history tours, dives, etc. Now you can generate income from any secret passion, skill, or knowledge that you have and want to share with the world. The best part is you do not have to invest a lot of capital into your idea to see if it works. You can leverage Airbnb's website and platform to advertise to customers. This is how you can test your idea with no advertising cost. Isn't that awesome?

Here are a few experiences that I have seen:

- **A sandwich feast:** $49 per person. A two-hour walking tour that includes sandwiches from multiple restaurants.

- **Play and cuddle with cats and kittens:** $18 per person for one hour.

- **Fishing in a park:** $55 per person for one and a half hours.

- **The rage cage:** You get to break printers, plates, and more with a bat. $45 per person for one hour. Equipment included.

- **Photo shoots in _____:** $35 for two hours per person.

Do you see how you can create any type of experience that you want and charge money for it? You have always been able to create and make money from these types of experiences. It was just harder and more expensive to build and test. This was before Airbnb made experiences so easy to create and share.

Let me give you an example I used to get paid to run. For those of you who wake up each morning and love to go for a run, God bless you. I am just not motivated that way. I wanted to stay in shape for soccer and knew I needed to do more running. But I still needed to find the right motivation to get myself to run three to six miles per run, multiple times per week. My friend Teran told me about one of her chiropractic friends who was starting a side business giving running tours in different cities. I thought if someone was going to pay me to run, then I could get motivated to run several times a week.

Would you exercise more if someone paid you?

I knew I would have to train on my own to build up my endurance to be able to talk and give a guided running tour at the same time. I was not paid a lot of money to do the running tours, but now I had the right motivation. (To be clear, I am not a fast runner and would only give tours to people who run at a slower pace. Other guides would take out the professional marathon or faster-paced runners.) People loved the tours, and you would be surprised at the number of sites and experiences you can have in a thirty- to sixty-minute run around NYC. For me, instead of paying for a gym membership or a personal trainer, I got paid to run and meet new people.

I know that 94.6 percent of you can turn your passion or something related to your passion into a revenue stream. I am not passionate about running, but I needed to run to support something I *am* passionate about—**soccer**.

What can you turn into a revenue-generating activity that can fuel your passion?

A lot of people are not passionate about investing in real estate, but they use the cash flow from their real estate to fund their charity or passions. You just want to make sure this activity is in line with your goals and dreams.

I was speaking at an event in Las Vegas and met a young woman who drove six-plus hours to be at the event. While I was signing a book for her, she said that she owned a dance studio for kids. She needed to generate some extra income to fund her studio, so she was thinking about becoming a real estate agent. There is nothing wrong with becoming a real estate agent.

I asked her, "What are you passionate about?"

"Teaching kids how to dance. I want to build a business by teaching kids after school and on the weekends to dance."

"You can 100 percent become an agent. But you understand you will have to get trained, and work evenings and weekends. It takes a significant amount of time to become a successful agent. Do you see how this conflicts with your goal of building a dance school for kids?"

She said, "Yes."

Sometimes we are so involved in our business that we cannot step back and see the ten-thousand-foot view. We are in survival/bootstrapping mode. Often coaches and mentors can better see the long view for your business.

I suggested instead that she partner with adult dance schools and restaurants, and leverage Airbnb by creating dance experiences for both adults and kids. She could also volunteer or apply to be a judge at dance competitions. As a judge, her status as a dance teacher would likely raise. Plus, all these activities would build brand awareness for her dance studio, which is her passion, and there would not be a lot of up-front marketing and advertising expenses.

Sometimes it just takes a few minutes of planning or working with a coach to set you on the right path towards your goals and dreams.

Now, it is your turn.

EXERCISE:
Turn Your Passions into Profits!

Do you want your answers in a digital format? If so, go to thelaunchbuttonbook.com and click the login button to create your own The Launch Button Blueprint for Success PDF!

- **What in your life can you convert from an expense to a revenue-generating activity?** An example could be that you are a good cook and should be cooking more healthy meals for your family, but you do not feel you have enough time. What if you started teaching a cooking class? You could teach people to cook, and generate revenue, while also preparing healthy and nutritional foods for your family.

- **Do a review of your financial situation and your current expenses. What can you create an experience from?**

- **What are you good at?**

- **What do you enjoy doing for fun?**

- **What are your hobbies?**

- **What do you not like to do but know you need to do or get better at?** This could be eating right, exercise, finances, meditation, etc.

- **What skill or experience do you want to master and teach other people?** The saying goes that you only master something when you are able to teach someone else the skill.

7

Creating a Blueprint for Your Future

Designing the life and lifestyle that you want. Are you bicoastal, bicontinental, or full nomad?

A LOT OF PEOPLE GO THROUGH LIFE MAKING FINANCIAL AND life choices based on their fears instead of taking steps to reach their goals. Nelson Mandela said, "May your choices reflect your hopes, not your fears."

Most people are not happy with their life plan. They dream of being able to travel and not being tied down to their job or a home. These people believe it is near impossible to change or reach their dream lifestyle because they do not have enough money in savings, a high enough credit score, and/or the income to get financing.

What if you could build your dream life? How much happier would you and your family be? What would that feel like to you?

Do you remember this diagram from Chapter One?

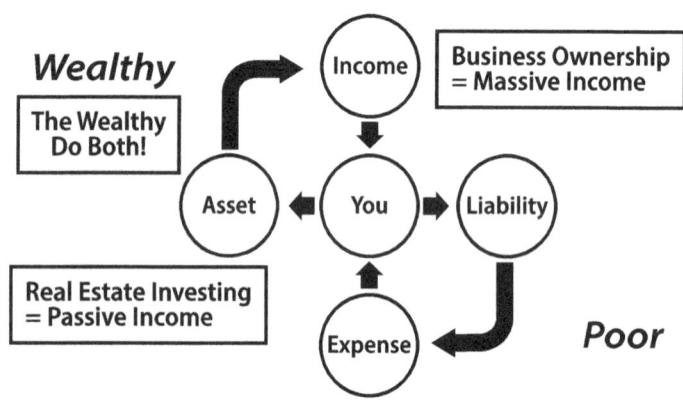

Assets vs. Liabilities

Make Money Twice and Then Spend it!

What if you could get your dream trips paid for without having to save for them each year? Say your dream trip is to travel to Australia and dive the Great Barrier Reef. Let's assume it costs

$10,000 for flight, hotel, etc. Instead of saving the money or using your credit cards to purchase the trip, you invest that money into a business or real estate deal that generates $1,000 a month. Ten months later, you have the funds to buy your trip to Australia. The best part is that when you get back from Australia, you have had an amazing experience and another $1,000 was deposited into your bank account. Now, you can plan a trip to Australia every ten months or to your next bucket-list place. It does not cost you anything extra. This is called "delayed gratification."

This same philosophy could be used to put your child through college so they can leave school debt-free. Student-loan debt is the second-largest debt in America today. This problem could be solved by using delayed gratification.

DEVELOPING A BLUEPRINT PLAN FOR YOUR LIFE

Most people never sit down and plan out how they want their life to be. They allow other outside influences to push them through the confines of their life. This is backward! You should define what you want in life and then find a job, start a business, and so on, that supports the lifestyle that you want.

Everyone has hopes and dreams, but to get what you want, you need to be really specific. When I speak at live events, people always come up to me and say, "I want more money." So, I give them a quarter, and I say, "I just fulfilled your life's goal of more money." This is what happens in life when you do not clearly define your goals and dreams.

Most people only have a job résumé, but Jesse Itzler talks about building a **life résumé**. The life résumé concept is about building experiences, creating memories, and doing more. What do you want on your life résumé? Do you want to be tied to a desk for over forty hours a week? I have taken this concept one step further—combine your life résumé with the blueprint plan for your business. I call it your **Blueprint Plan for Success**. Let's start to clearly define your plan for success!

Pull out a sheet of paper and write down all of the things that you have achieved in your life that you are proud of and want the world to know about. This should include your personal life, business, and so forth. Take a few minutes, set this book aside, and write these accomplishments out for yourself. Simply by making this list, you will open up your mind to all sorts of possibilities. Even after you are done making this list, you will continue to come up with additional ideas. Keep your list with you for the next few days.

Great job in starting your list. Now, let's better define your Blueprint Plan for Success!

- **Personal Life:** In an ideal world where money is not a concern, explain in more detail what you want.

  * Would you be single, married, or other?

  * Do you want to have kids or not?

  * If you do want kids, how many? How many boys and girls?

* Do you want to have any pets? What type of pets and how many?

* Do you have a car or cars? How many cars? What type of cars do you want to own?

* Do you own your own home? Is it in a city? Is it in a suburb? Is it near a lake, a beach, a mountain?

* Do you have a second or third home? Is it in a city? Is it in a suburb? Is it near a lake, a beach, a mountain?

* Do you volunteer/serve or give back to charity? What do you do to volunteer? How often do you volunteer or serve? How much do you donate each year?

* Do you work out? How many times a week?

* Which activities do you do and how many times a week?

* Do you pray or meditate? For how long? How many times a week?

* How many fun/vacation trips do you take each year? How many times do you travel a year? What are the places on your bucket list that you want to visit?

* What are some things on your bucket list that you
  want to do or experience?

* What other things do you want on your life
  résumé?

* How much monthly revenue do you feel you will
  need to support this lifestyle?

Now that you have a clearer picture of what you want your ideal
life to look like, you can make your decisions about taking a job,
starting a business, investing in real estate, being in a relationship, or anything else that supports your ideal life. Every time
you are offered an opportunity, you are going to compare it to the
answers in your life's blueprint. If the new opportunity supports
your dream life 75 percent or more, then you should accept the
opportunity. If it does not, then you will turn down the opportunity. This will make your decisions in life easier and less stressful,
and save you a lot of time trying to figure out the right thing to do.

Throughout my corporate and entrepreneurial career, I have
been able to build my life résumés while on business trips. One of
my favorites was when I got an opportunity to travel to Australia
for my corporate job and turned it into an opportunity to scuba
dive the Great Barrier Reef. I had always wanted to learn how
to scuba dive and this trip forced me to learn quickly. In fact, I
had to do my training dives in a cold NYC pool during the winter.
Then, when I got to Australia, I only had to pass my open water
diver exam and get certified. I understood this could be a once-
in-a-lifetime opportunity, and I was not going to miss it. After
working a day in Sydney, my buddy Joey and I flew to Cairns
to dive the Great Barrier Reef. Joey was already certified. I still

had to do my open water dives. I quickly passed my certification dives and then joined Joey and the rest of the qualified divers. It was an amazing experience. We stayed overnight on the reef and did a night dive. The sea life was amazing, and it was a once-in-a-lifetime experience!

One other important fact is that what we focus on is what we achieve. The best way to focus on something is to track it. That is why I have created a five-week productivity journal to help you build the steps to your dream life. It will track your daily habits so you can achieve what you want in your life. Just go to hughzaretsky.com and click on books or go to Amazon and search for *"The Steps to Fire Your Boss - 5 Week Productivity Journal"* or "Hugh Zaretsky" to order it.

DEVELOPING A BUSINESS/WORK BLUEPRINT THAT SUPPORTS YOUR LIFE BLUEPRINT = SUCCESS!

Once you have your life blueprint, now we can develop your work or business blueprint. The question is: do you need to make a major change in your job to be able to start a business and/or invest in real estate? The answer is...it depends. Your job may cause you stress and take up a lot of your time, but you can use it to launch your dream business or build the cash flow. However, most people come home from work and say they are exhausted and do not have time to build their dreams.

Remember the exercise we did earlier in the book about words having energy? Let's do it again to reinforce your wording. Are you ready?

- The statement I want you to say out loud is: "I am exhausted."

- What happened to your body and your energy?

- Say it again and pay attention to your body and your energy.

- What did you notice? Did you notice yourself getting smaller and your energy dropping? Most people will feel their shoulders slump, their stomach and lower back round down, and their energy level drop. Did you feel that in your body?

- Now, I want you to do the same exercise, but this time say out loud, "I have so many opportunities to make money!"

- Say it again.

- What changes did you notice in your body?

Most people will notice their chest puffing out, their shoulders and lower back straightening, and they will feel themselves standing taller and feeling excited with more energy. You might feel exhausted when you get home from work and have to work on your side hustle late at night. Or, you can feel excited after work because your side hustle gives you so many more opportunities to make money. The choice is up to you. This is called reassociation.

Just about every successful entrepreneur and real estate investor had to start working their side hustle in the evening and on weekends. In the beginning, it is what you do anytime between

8:00 p.m. and 8:00 a.m. that determines if your business is going to be successful or not. If all of your energy is drained by your job, then you will not feel like building your business in the evening or on the weekends. So the reassociation that you need to do is: "I choose to work my job at _____ so I can fund my entrepreneurial business about _____. That way, I will never have to work a job in the future."

Your business blueprint is also important to help you stay on track in your business, just like your life plan is important for staying on track in your life. It is also an important part of raising capital to support your business and for eventually hiring employees and/or taking on investors. You should also develop a marketing plan for your business. Your marketing plan will focus on generating leads and promote your business to the world. Let's start with your business plan.

- Do you know what type of entrepreneurial business you want to start?

If the answer is no, then...

- What are you passionate about?

- Whatever that is, then you need to find people who started a business in that field.

- Do you want to dedicate your life to volunteering or a cause?

If so, then you may want to learn how to invest in real estate so you can build up your passive income to support your lifestyle.

Then you will be able to volunteer all of your time.

If you still do not know what you want to do, then go to the eFramily Ohana at eFramily.com for more resources or schedule a one-on-one consultation at hughzaretsky.com.

If the answer is yes, then clearly define your business and/or real estate investment plan, your ideal future in more detail, and what you want your business to be like.

- Do you want to build a big, midsize, or small business?

- Do you want lots of employees? 1099 contractors?

- What is your gross revenue goal for your company?

- Ideally, would you want to work from home or an office?

- Are you a good work-from-home person or not?

- Do you want to be in or near a big city?

- Do you want to be near the beach, mountains, or a lake?

- Do you want to be able to work from anywhere? Bicoastal? Internationally? Full nomad?

- What type of investment properties do you want to own? Single-family? Two- to four-family properties? Multifamily (five to one hundred unit) buildings? Commercial property?

- What do you want your monthly passive income revenue to be?

- Do you want to manage the properties or hire a property manager?

- Do you want traditional rental properties or vacation-style rentals (Airbnb, VRBO, etc.)?

There are additional things that you may want to consider that are appropriate for your specific business when you are creating your plan.

One important thing to consider as you are developing both your business and life blueprints is taxes. These apply to both your business and personal life. Every state, city, and even counties or townships have different taxable rates. It is important that as you design your life and business you understand what your taxed rate will be. A lot of people like to open their business and/or make their primary residence in Florida, Tennessee, Texas, Wyoming, or Nevada. Why? Because you typically will pay less in taxes and you'll be able to keep more of your money.

IT IS AMAZING WHAT A FEW MILES CAN DO TO REDUCE YOUR TAXES

Historically, New York, California, and New Jersey are some of the most heavily taxed states. I have been told by several CPAs that it would be cheaper for me from a tax perspective to move to Florida, Texas, or Puerto Rico and commute via airplane to New

York City because of state and city taxes. It's important you check with your CPA, because laws and taxes are constantly changing.

Twice in my life, I have almost moved to the Carolinas. The second time, I was prepared to move but I felt I still needed to keep my office in New York City. Therefore, I wanted an easy commute by plane, and Charlotte, North Carolina, appeared like the perfect location. It was a rapidly growing city, had a lot of direct flights to NYC, and the flight's time was less than two hours. This would make commuting each week easy. As I learned more about the area, it became clear that I could reduce my taxes further by living in South Carolina. If you are not familiar with Charlotte, then this sounds far away. Your mind automatically registers that this is a different state. So it must be far away. If you know the Charlotte area, then you know some of the suburbs of Charlotte are in South Carolina. People from North Carolina go to South Carolina to shop for clothing because the taxes are cheaper. The South Carolina suburbs also boast some of the top-rated schools in the area. Why not live in the lower-taxed state from the start? My commute time would have been very similar. Unfortunately, due to personal reasons, I did not make the move. However, you can see that a few miles can make a big difference in your tax savings each year, and they compound over time.

You will want to meet with your CPA or tax professional and ask them some questions regarding your business plan. Here are a few examples:

- What is your current state income tax rate?

- Are there additional city taxes in the city where you want to work or live?

- Are there any unique tax deductions offered by that city or state?

- Does your city or state have additional taxes they charge business owners?

- Are there any additional real estate taxes?

Now, it is time for you to take *action* and design your life and business plan. This is something that you should always keep with you because it will help you make decisions faster in life. These two plans will keep evolving over time, so you want to keep updating them.

EXERCISE:
Design Your Blueprint Plan for Success!

Do you want your answers in a digital format? If so, go to thelaunchbuttonbook.com and click the login button to create your own The Launch Button Blueprint for Success PDF!

1. Go back to the questions above about your life and answer them in detail.

2. Go to the questions above about building a business that supports the lifestyle that you want and answer them.

3. Start brainstorming ideas about what you are passionate about.

4. Meet with your CPA to discuss places where you want to live and the tax benefits.

5. If you haven't started filling out your Blueprint Plan yet, now is the time to get started.

8

Understanding the Entrepreneur Roller Coaster

Entrepreneurial Roller Coaster of Emotions

Protecting you from you. Plus, preparing your mind for the journey to success while breaking down business and real estate misconceptions.

I WANT TO PREPARE YOUR MIND FOR THE JOURNEY TO SUCCESS as well as to protect you from yourself. I need you to prepare for the entrepreneur emotional roller coaster and what successful entrepreneurs have done to get through it. Most people only ever see the final result on TV, the internet, or in a magazine. David Goggins calls it "callus your mind." They do *not* see the years of hard work that someone has put in behind the scenes. What is the entrepreneur emotional roller coaster?

THE NUMBER ONE CAUSE FOR PEOPLE QUITTING THEIR JOBS

Emotion.

The entrepreneur emotional roller coaster is driven by the emotional swings that come with being an entrepreneur. These highs and lows can come from many different things. The scenario usually plays out like this: You put your blood, sweat, and tears into something and are super excited to launch it. Then you see it crash and burn. This could be launching your business, a new product or service, a big sale, interview, or podcast. It can even be something as simple as getting excited because you have invited a person to a meeting and then they do not show up. These highs and lows are part of the journey to success. Most entrepreneurs have failed hundreds if not thousands of times before they achieved success.

> *"I have tried 99 times and failed, but on the 100th time came success."*

—ALBERT EINSTEIN

For most people, the hardest thing to adjust to when they leave 50x40x40 is not getting a consistent paycheck every two weeks. Being an entrepreneur sounds awesome until you experience your first emotional letdown due to potential loss of income. Once this happens, your brain starts to crave the comfort of your old job. That is why you will often hear people leave a job to start a business, then fail and go back to getting a job. Sometimes you need to fail two, three, or even more times before you get it right. Like in a movie, this is the hero's journey that you must take!

In the beginning, the emotional roller coaster swings go from super high to super low, and I have seen the entrepreneur emotional roller coaster cause lots of entrepreneurs to quit on their dreams. You might be excited about the launch of a new product, book, business, getting guests to a meeting, or being invited to speak at an event. Then your launch gets canceled or delayed, no one shows up for your event, etc. You go from super high about your business to super low. Sometimes this can happen several times in a single day. Over time, your emotions will smooth out, and you will get used to these swings.

I am sitting at a hotel on a beach near the Panama Canal on the Gulf of Panama. The tide here is a perfect analogy for the entrepreneur emotional roller coaster. There are some oceanic forces that cause the tide here to drop over twenty feet in depth from high to low tide. The real phenomenon is that twenty feet of depth causes the water to pull back about three hundred feet from the beach. I shot a video to show the difference between high and low tide. The reason I share this with you is because most people only see successful entrepreneurs as the finished product on stage or TV. This is just like the tide washing up on the pretty, sandy beaches of Panama. You do not often see the mud, small pools of water that fish get caught in, or the jagged rocks. These are similar to the trials of a person's hero journey that they had to go through in life before they became successful.

The rocks, mud, and small pools of water all symbolize the internal stories in your head, your limiting beliefs, your weaknesses, and your fears. Surprisingly, these may include some of the people in your life. Your entrepreneur journey will expose things to you that you did not even know you were afraid of.

The rising tide in Panama takes consistent daily action to smooth out the jagged edges of the rocks. This does not happen overnight. It takes weeks, months, and years of the water working daily to round the jagged edges. This is the same process that we must all go through during the entrepreneur journey to round ourselves into the best version of us.

The two main things that typically cause emotional swings on your journey are your feelings and your finances. You get super high and super low. Let me tell you a secret. Most days, you will not feel like doing the things you need to do to build your business. It is the same with whatever you want to achieve. However, it is your ability to take consistent daily actions (CDA) whether you feel like it or not that will make you successful in life. This is true for your health, wealth, relationships, and success in life.

Some people call this the "power of habit." I do not like this phrase, because when you break a habit, it takes at least twenty-one days to rebuild your habit. However, consistency can be built day by day. Plus, you can reestablish consistency in only two days. I say all the time, "Consistency beats skill each and every day."

You can get back on track in only two days instead of twenty-one days by starting a new streak. You are going to have a family vacation day, a day of travel, or worse, a bad day that gets you down. Well, the next day, you can get right back to doing the things that you need to do to be consistent. The saying goes, "Get back up on the horse." It's true!

CONCEPT: NO ONE CAN DO ANYTHING TO YOU

Most days, as an entrepreneur, you do not feel like doing what you need to do. You do not have the luxury as an entrepreneur, especially in the beginning, to take days or even weeks off. You need to push through the emotions and do what you need to do. The fastest way to do this is to get out of your head and take action.

One concept you can use to help protect your emotions is to understand that no one can do anything *to* you. You have to allow them to do it to you. This will help you to take responsibility and allow you to change your emotions if someone offends you. Here is how to become unoffendable:

1. Ask yourself why that statement offended you.

2. Ask the other person to clarify what they meant. Most times, you will realize they did not mean the statement the way you interpreted it.

CONCEPT: BECOMING WORLD-CLASS TAKES TIME AND CDA

You need to give yourself enough time to develop your skills to become world-class, and it will always take way longer than you expect. By remembering to give yourself permission to suck (we covered this earlier in this book), every time you try something new, you will continue to learn and eventually become world-class at the new skill. Just be patient with yourself.

Financial Stress

Financial stress is also one of the biggest issues for entrepreneurs in the beginning. It takes time to get used to the ebb and flow of your entrepreneur business income. This is why it is important that you have a reserve account set up to cover downturns. Eventually, the ebb and flow smooths out, and your brain adjusts to your rolling finances.

The number one cause of divorce is financial stress. When one person in a relationship feels insecure financially or fears they are going to lose their home, it tends to spiral into other areas of their life. You should set up your "Oh Crap Account" and fund it before you leave your job.

The Oh Crap Account

The Oh Crap Account is meant to reduce your financial stress after you push the launch button and fire your boss. This should be an account you do not see when you look at your checking or savings account. The easiest way is to put this account in a different bank or financial institution. You must also decide how much money you need in your Oh Crap Account or how many months of bills you want covered. It should be fully funded before you leave your job.

This is a benefit for you (and your partner if you are in a relationship) because it provides a safety net if things get hairy financially. In most of the relationships I have observed, there is one person who is more conservative with their finances and feels secure knowing they have X number of months in savings and will not lose their home in a downturn or emergency. I only know of one relationship where both parties were willing to jump in without a safety net and fluctuate financially from broke to wealthy. Most people understand that their life will be less stressful if their significant other feels secure and supports the new entrepreneurial and/or real estate business. This is one tool you can use to help the more conservative party feel financially secure and reduce the stress in your life.

The question I get next is, "How many months of expenses should I have in my Oh Crap Account?" The answer usually is three to six months, but for some people, it will be a year. COVID has been a great test for people who had their Oh Crap Accounts funded. This has been the first time some traditional businesses, restaurants, etc. have been shut down and generated zero dollars in monthly revenue. Unfortunately, a lot of small- and medium-sized businesses will go under and never come back, because they did not have a big enough reserve in their Oh Crap Account. I do not want this to happen to you.

Understand this account does not have to be all in cash. It could be two months in cash, one month in precious metals, and two months cash available in an overfunded life insurance policy. There are lots of different investment options for you to consider. However, you want these funds in a very conservative investment. One that you can quickly convert to cash in an emergency.

STRESS CAUSES US TO MAKE BAD DECISIONS

Often, when we are under financial or emotional duress, we make shortsighted decisions to just get by. When you look back on those decisions, you usually realize that they were not the best long-term financial decisions for you but were made out of necessity. So, your Oh Crap Account will also allow you to stay out of the shortsighted decision trap.

When we are stressed out financially, we tend to hold our breath. This does not allow our brain to get the oxygen it needs to function properly. This causes us to make bad or shortsighted decisions. The Navy SEALs have a breathing technique that they do before they go into a stressful situation. It allows them to remain calm and make good decisions under pressure.

1. Inhale for a count of four.

2. Hold your breath for a count of four.

3. Exhale for a count of four.

4. Wait for a count of four before inhaling.

You will be amazed at the amount of stress and anxiety that will disappear after doing that exercise four times.

STAYING EVEN-KEELED

Your objective is to stay even-keeled like a ship cutting through the ocean. I want you to always be cautiously optimistic. This will help keep you grounded. I have watched a lot of entrepreneurs crash and burn from the emotional roller coaster. That is why I train people to make sure they have multiple streams of income and three exit plans on each real estate deal.

Would Losing a $170 Million Deal Cause You to Become Emotional?

You will have failures and learning experiences in your entrepreneur business and in your real estate career. The bigger the deal, the smaller the issue that may cause it to fall apart.

I have used this philosophy myself when I thought I had put together a deal to sell a $170 million hotel in NYC only to have it fall apart. A 1 percent payout on that deal was worth $1.7 million, but while I worked on it, I never allowed myself to start spending the money in my head. I continued working on other real estate deals instead. I knew that it took only one problem, market change, COVID, etc. for the entire deal to collapse. This is one of the few deals that I could not put back together.

Note: In general, the bigger the deal, the smaller the issue that may cause it to fall apart.

That is why you need to stay even-keeled. For some people, losing $1.7 million would cause them to go into a tailspin and could tank their entire business or fortune. In poker, they call this "going on tilt." Why? If a player loses a big hand they thought they were going to win, and they get pissed off about it, more than likely they will overbet the next several hands and dump their stacks—the rest of their poker chips. When you go on tilt, you play poorly because you are being influenced by your emotions. In real life, the same thing happens. People have already spent their commissions in their head, stopped working on other deals, and/or counted on that money to pay their bills.

I stayed cautiously optimistic that the $170 million deal would close throughout the process, until I realized it was finally dead. Then I moved on and focused on my other businesses. Other people involved allowed it to become emotional. They tried many times to salvage the deal only to waste more time and resources. This eventually caused them to give up on their hopes and dreams. Worse, they became emotionally tied to the deal and it affected their personal relationships as well.

Do you see how your emotions and going on tilt can possibly put you in a financial hole? That could take days or years to recover from.

A SINGLE PHONE CALL CAN CHANGE YOU FROM QUITTING TO MAKING $20,000 IN A MONTH

Most people have read Napoleon Hill's book and know the story of stopping three feet from gold. If you have not read it, get the book *Think and Grow Rich*. You can find it for free online or go to hughzaretsky.com/books to get a free copy. I have seen this happen many, many times with different people on my team. Let me give you just one of a hundred examples from my students.

I have worked closely with one of my eFramily members over the past fifteen years. Before we started working together, though, this member had never done a real estate deal. In her first year working with my team, she did five real estate transactions and built a $250,000-plus real estate investing company.

While her real estate business was taking off like gangbusters, she was not having the same success with her entrepreneur business and building a team. She was ready to quit. She sent me a text message basically saying so. I asked her to schedule a call with me, and she did. On the call, she told me all the victim excuses she had built up in her head. She explained "why" she was not good at being an entrepreneur, and she wanted to stick to investing in real estate. She was in full victim mentality mode.

I had to snap her out of it. We did a reassociation (as I demonstrated earlier in this book), and after the call, she felt better and was willing to give the entrepreneur business another try. About nine days later, she put in a sales order that generated her a $10,000 check. Two months after that, she had a $20,000 week. Before the call, she was ready to quit. Because she did not, she generated an extra $30,000 in a few short months.

That is why I tell all my students, "You will quit on you before I will quit on you." I have been riding the entrepreneur roller coaster since 2005, and I am not getting off anytime soon. It is just way too much fun.

Would You Like a "Stop Me from Quitting" Phone Call?

Bonus: I will give you a free bonus for purchasing this book, which is the ability to schedule one "stop me from quitting call" for FREE. You will need to fill out a questionnaire first so I can maximize our time together and coordinate the call. I have saved hundreds, if not thousands, of people from quitting on their lifelong dreams and goals by this one single phone call. Go to hughzaretsky.com and click "Start Here" for your one free "Stop Me from Quitting" phone call.

You can always quit. The hardest thing is to push through when you feel like quitting. That is why I say, "Quitting is the easiest thing you can do, so why quit now?" You can quit tomorrow or after ten more calls and just keep pushing it further and further out.

EXERCISE:
Staying in the Game

Do you want your answers in a digital format? If so, go to thelaunchbuttonbook.com and click the login button to create your own The Launch Button Blueprint for Success PDF!

- **Which podcast or videos will bring you inspiration or keep you going?**

  * Go to hughzaretsky.com/podcast or YouTube to get the latest podcasts. You can follow Hugh Zaretsky or ShitWillHappen. Make sure to click the *follow* buttons and turn the notifications on. This way, you get updated when a new podcast or video drops. I interview entrepreneurs and let them tell their stories about how they overcame crap in their life to become successful entrepreneurs. Some of these stories will shock you!

- **What state do I want to remain in?**

- Practice, practice, practice these exercises to get you out of a bad frame of mind.

- **Take action:** Get out of your head and into your body to change your brain chemicals.

- **What physical activity can you do when you get stressed?**

- **What does "staying even-keeled and taking control of your emotions" mean to you?**

- No one can do anything *to* you. You have to allow them to do it to you. This will enable you to change your emotions if someone offends you. Here is how to become unoffendable:

  * **Ask yourself why that statement offended you?**

  * Ask the other person to clarify what they meant. Most times, you will realize they did not mean the statement the way you interpreted it.

- The Navy SEALs breathing technique. Repeat four times. You will be amazed at the amount of stress and anxiety that will disappear.

  * Inhale for a count of four.

  * Hold your breath for a count of four.

  * Exhale for a count of four.

  * Wait for a count of four before inhaling.

9

Your Rocket Fuel

*Get Outside the Box and
Unconventional Financing*

INVESTMENT PROJECT

-Call Key Contacts

-Introduce Project

-Line Up Funds
(Other people's money)

Your Rocket Fuel of Cash Flow

Financing is wide open. You no longer need great income, perfect credit, etc. to get funding for your business. Funding is the rocket fuel for your business.

EVERYONE WILL NEED FUNDING FOR THEIR BUSINESS AND real estate transactions, so it is important that you understand how to set yourself up to get it. Funding is the fuel that will allow your business to launch and grow or crash and burn. There are many nontraditional places where we can find funding in today's world, and we will discuss a few in more detail in this chapter. Most people start out having to "bootstrap" the funding for their business to get it off the ground before people will invest in it. If you have ever watched *Shark Tank*, you will notice one of the questions the sharks ask just about every time is, "How much of your own money did you invest?" Below are a couple of the more popular ways to get funding for your business and goals.

PAY YOURSELF FIRST

Before we get into the funding options, one thing I need to make sure you are doing is paying yourself first. It is important to pay yourself first. How do you do this? Simply, take some money each month and put it into a startup account before you pay your bills. You can use this money to fund your business, reinvest in it, or fund an investment. Most people do it the opposite way and pay themselves last. That is why they never get ahead. Paying yourself first and reinvesting that money requires discipline and will start to build good financial habits. Pick a percentage of your income to use to start building your startup account. Some people start with 5 percent, 10 percent, or 15 percent.

Let's assume you get paid $5,000 a month after taxes. What paying yourself first means is you would take 10 percent or $500 and put it into your startup account. You would then live off of and make other investments with the other $4,500. You repeat this each pay cycle.

If you build this habit now, then when you have your business, it will be even easier, because you will always have to set money aside for business upgrades, technology, cell phones, expansion, etc. The "paying yourself first" mentality will always leave you with a pool of cash to use.

Now, let's cover some of the more common funding options.

Bootstrapping

Bootstrapping your business means building a business from the ground up using your personal savings and financing. You then reinvest the cash from your sales back into the business. This term comes from the 1800s when people said, "Pull yourself up by your bootstraps." This is the way that most entrepreneurs start their first or several businesses. They want to prove their idea works before they get family, friends, and investors involved.

The problem with this is it limits your speed of growth and expansion because it is restricted by your free cash flow. This typically slows down your speed of production and/or how fast you can get your product or service to the market. (I will give you a strategy later in the chapter to help free up your cash flow and save you $1,000 to $100,000 in interest payments you already agreed to pay the bank.) The more free cash flow you have, the faster your business can grow.

Creative Financing Strategies

Creative financing strategies are usually needed when you do not have either money or credit. You are no longer restricted to just traditional banks in order to raise money. In today's world, we have so many different avenues for raising capital: from crowdsourcing sites like Kickstarter, to private investors, 401(k) s/IRAs, whole life insurance, and hard money lenders, just to name a few. There are lenders for all different industries, businesses, and real estate transactions. You just need to match the right lender with your terms and access to capital. Do not worry as much about the interest rate. In the bonus section, I will show you how to greatly reduce the interest rate.

Business Lenders

Business lenders lend you a percentage of your receivables or credit card processing income. They will look at your historic trends and give you a chunk of money based on your billed receivables. Their rates and terms will vary, so you need to read all of the documentation and the terms of the loan. Some will do a flat loan, and some will do a revolving line of credit.

Real Estate Deals

Remember the twenty-one-plus strategies and government programs from Chapter Five? These can help you acquire or buy your own home. You can use these to invest in real estate. These strategies will be explained in further detail in another book, complete with deals, stories, and strategies. I will explore some of my favorite strategies in each area here.

Subject To

This is the ability to take over the payments for someone else's mortgage with full disclosure from the bank that holds the mortgage. Since you are not applying for a mortgage, your credit score usually does not matter. The bank just wants to know you can afford to make the monthly payments.

Lease Option

This is the ability to rent a property for a period of time *before* you purchase the property at an agreed-upon price in the future and before a certain date. This allows you to build or fix your credit while also potentially rehabbing the property or fixing it up. This way, when you go to buy it, you already have prebuilt equity in the deal. This can make it easier to get financing in the future.

Short-Term Rentals/Airbnb

If you do not actually want to own a property in today's shared economy, there are some strategies that will still allow you to generate income without owning the property. One of those is called "lease and re-lease." This has become a popular strategy with some people who want to rent properties on Airbnb, VRBO, or other vacation rental sites.

Short-term rentals is one of the fastest-growing (and currently the trendiest) strategies for investing in real estate. It is so new the laws keep changing. Therefore, it is up to you to stay up to date with the laws. If you are going to use this strategy, make sure you have two backup plans in case the market or laws change. I teach all of my students to go into each deal with three exit strategies (your primary plus two backup plans), in case something like COVID happens again. That is why my students and Ohana are prepared for any Black Swan event.

Some people are leasing properties and re-leasing them on short-term rental platforms. You do not even need to qualify for a mortgage; you just need to be able to qualify to rent an apartment. This can make things much easier for you to get started in the real estate investing business. There can be a lower cost of entry from a financing perspective. Instead of saving up for a down payment, you typically need the first month's rent, last month's rent, and a month or two of security. This means there is no excuse for you not to get started!

I want to make sure you do everything ethically and legally, which means giving the landlord full disclosure up front about the purpose for leasing the property and your intentions to re-lease. This will require a rider or a modification to the landlord's standard lease. This is why you should have a real estate attorney on your team. To learn more about real estate investing, go to eFramily.com or hughzaretsky.com.

The worst thing you can do is to violate the lease and cause the landlord to throw all of your furniture out on the street. Depending on the state, this can happen in as little as a week to a maximum of thirty days. Save yourself the potential legal headache and disclose everything up front and in writing. Make sure to get the landlord to sign off on the addendum, modified lease, etc. This way you protect yourself and your cash flow.

Using Your Personal Line of Credit (PLOC)

Some people will leverage their personal credit options with traditional banks to fund their business. Most people do not realize that once you fire your boss it is harder to get traditional funding for your business and real estate investing. I did not think about this when I left the corporate world. So learn from my mistake. Most traditional bank loans and lines of credit want you to have W-2 income and a history of steady income. Once you fire your boss, you no longer have two years of steady income, which can make you a credit risk. Therefore, you want to make sure you have secured all of the lines of credit and loans you need before leaving the corporate world. This also includes zero-percent credit cards. It can take six months to two years to build up your track record with the banks again.

This is why you will want a strategic plan on how to apply for loans, lines of credit, and credit cards before you leave your job. The longer your time frame, the easier it is to plan out your application process. Traditional mortgages and lines of credits (PLOCs and HELOCs) can take thirty to sixty days to be approved. Credit cards take a much shorter amount of time to be approved. Remember, inquires on your credit score can cause it to drop temporarily.

Build and Use Business Credit

I am not an expert on building business credit, but it does take some time to create credit history for your business. You can build it faster if you have good personal credit. If you have bad personal credit, it will take longer to build business credit, but it is still possible.

Just like anything else, you can build your own business credit or hire a company to build it for you. If you hire a company, make sure you do your research on them first. If you need some recommendations, go to the resources section on my website at hughzaretsky.com/resources. There are a few things that will help you build business credit, such as:

- You want to have a separate business telephone number. You can use Google Voice or another service.

- You want a business address that is not your home. A PO box is not the best idea for this. There are a lot of shared office spaces where you can get a box, be able to use a conference room, and pay one monthly fee to get everything that you need. I will go into more details on shared office spaces and services in Chapter Ten.

Partners, Private Lenders, or Hard Money Lenders

These lenders typically require either higher interest rates and/or equity in your business. This is what the TV show *Shark Tank* is all about. If you want to use private lenders like friends and family, then you want to keep the limit to eight private investors or less. If they are set up properly, then they can use their 401(k)/IRA money to fund your business, real estate transactions, etc. If it is good enough for Mitt Romney to build a $100 million IRA, then it is good enough for you and your private investors (Cohan 2012). Romney hired people who understood how these laws work and so can you. In this book, you are learning some of the same secrets.

You can do all sorts of things with small groups of investors. However, if you want to have more investors and raise more funds, then you will need to move to a crowdfunding platform, create a **Private Placement Memorandum** (PPM), or create a private fund. A PPM and private fund will require you to hire an attorney to draw up the proper paperwork, which must be filed with the Securities and Exchange Commission (SEC). Depending on the law, you might also have to register this in each state where you have an investor. The startup cost is going to be higher. If you use a crowdsourcing site, they will charge you a percentage of the funds raised but will also do a lot of the paperwork for you. The choice is up to you.

There are lots of things you will need to create and/or build when you are first starting a business: your website, your sales funnel, marketing your business, product development, real estate, etc. In the early stages of a business, this often can be one of the more difficult times to get traditional bank financing. They typically want two years of income before they will give you a loan. This is why you may need to go to alternative sources.

Your Blueprint Plan for Success (life and business), which we created in Chapter Seven, will help you focus on the right ending strategy.

DO NOT BE FOOLED BY INTEREST RATES— AMORTIZED VERSUS SIMPLE INTEREST

People are often brainwashed into worrying about the interest rate of the loan. Banks spend millions of dollars advertising low interest rates. To me, the interest rate *does not matter.* In my opinion, the type of loan matters, and how fast you can receive the funds to invest into your business or real estate deal matters.

Most people do not understand that not all interest is created equal. There are typically two types of loans. There are **amortized loans** and **simple interest loans**. Each one applies interest in a different way or on a different scale. For example, we know there are two different scales that people use to tell temperature, right? Fahrenheit or Celsius. I was flying to Hawaii in the winter and was sitting next to an English couple, and they were talking about English summers back home. I asked them what the usual temperature was. They said around thirty-two degrees. My first thought was, *Wow, that is cold.* But then I remembered they were referring to Celsius. I had to translate the scale in my head, which is about eighty-nine degrees Fahrenheit. Do you understand how two numbers can mean different things based on a scale? Therefore, you have to know the scale more than the interest rate.

WHICH SCALE DOES YOUR LOAN USE?

Let's break down **amortized loans** and **simple interest loans** so you can understand the scale.

Amortized loans are front-loaded with interest. For example, on a traditional thirty-year mortgage it usually takes between sixteen to twenty years before half of your payment starts going to principal. That means for the first sixteen to twenty years, the majority of your payment goes toward interest.

The word "amortized" comes from the French word meaning, "to pay until you die." Some examples of amortized loans are mortgages, student loans, and car loans. Any amortized loan is usually front-loaded with interest.

If you want an eye-opening experience, go to Google and type in "mortgage amortization calculator." Choose a calculator and enter the data for your loan. Then, click "show" or "print" the amortization schedule. You will see that you end up paying a crap ton more in interest than you thought you would have. A simple cheat calculation that some people use is to multiply your amortized interest rate by twenty and that equals about how much you will pay in interest.

Is this fair, you ask? Yes. Why? Because you signed the loan document and agreed to the terms that were originally given to you. That is why it is important that you do the math. Sometimes it is cheaper to borrow money at 21 percent simple interest than 6 percent amortized interest. Now that you understand you are paying a crap ton more in interest than you thought, are you ready to learn and have financial discipline?

Simple interest loans are calculated on the average daily balance. Simple interest loans are lines of credit like HELOC, **Business Line of Credit** (BLOC), PLOC, and credit cards. Unfortunately, some people think credit cards are bad. Credit cards do not have a personality. They just bring out your financial discipline or lack thereof. The nice thing about most simple interest loans is that they are revolving, and you can use them over and over again.

A lot of people growing up hear "Credit cards are bad" or "Money is the root of all evil." This is victim talk from people who do not have financial discipline. You do not have a "bad credit card" like a devil sitting on one of your shoulders saying in your ear, "Use me to buy bad things!" and on the other shoulder a "good credit card" with an angel saying, "Use me to buy good things and make investments!" Credit cards and money do *not* have personalities. It is not money or credit cards that are bad. They just bring out *your* financial personality and discipline. If you do not have any financial discipline, then you will get in trouble using credit cards and lines of credit. Go back and read Dave Ramsey's or Suzy Orman's books to learn financial discipline and come back to this section.

DO YOU HAVE A GREAT DEPRESSION MINDSET?

Most people learned how to pay their bills from their parents, who learned from *their* parents. It goes all the way back to the twenties and the Great Depression. This is why some people have what I call a "Great Depression mindset" in today's world. This is the mentality of "save your money and then spend it" or "save your money and spend it twice by going into credit card debt." I want to introduce a new concept to some of you and present a way to pay for debt with debt, and then use your cash flow to get out of debt. I know it sounds weird, but this is the secret of the wealthy and how to get out of debt or pay off amortized loans in potentially a third of the time. Once you understand this concept, you cannot unlearn it. It can be a very powerful concept to pay off debt quickly.

This is an advanced wealth-building strategy that I am about to show you that does require you to exercise financial discipline. I want you to be fully informed so you can make the best decisions for you. I trust that you are a grown-arse adult and willing to take responsibility for your financial life. If you do not have financial discipline, this strategy is *not* for you! Skip this section and go to the next chapter.

I first learned about this strategy for quickly paying off debt back in 2007. During the housing crash of 2008–2010, some people lost their homes because of the risky part of this strategy. Aggressive strategies can save you more money in interest, but they also bring more risk. You could potentially lose your home or favorite property. That is why I like a modified version of the strategy that most places do not teach. My friend and longtime real estate investor, Tony Scotty, named it "chunking." This interest-reduction strategy protects you during a market crash and allows you to pay off your debts in one-third to two-thirds the time, while still saving you a crap ton in interest payments. Plus, you do not risk losing your home or your favorite investment property in a market crash.

In today's world, most people make decisions based on a monthly payment that fits within their monthly budget. As long as the monthly payment for your house, car, student loan, etc. fits within your budget, you accept the loan terms, often without reading all of the documents. People do not actually do the math and calculate that they are ultimately going to pay double the amount of their loan. This is why a 20 percent simple interest credit card isn't bad if you are using it the right way compared to an effective 40 percent to 120 percent amortized loan. We can create a plan to pay off the loan faster and save you a ton of money in interest payments.

To make this strategy work, you need four things:

1. You need a tool: a **Line of Credit** (LOC).

2. You need to pick one debt at a time that you want to attack for a period of time.

3. You need to be cash-flow positive or neutral.

4. You have your Oh Crap Account set up because you are going to stop putting money in savings during this process.

Once you have identified these items, then it is a simple formula that involves repeating the process until you have chunked down the debt that you want to attack.

Step 1: Get Ready

First you need to free up your tool. This requires you to take all of your income each month and deposit or transfer it to your LOC. In essence, you make your line of credit your checking account. Remember, the interest is calculated on "average daily balance."

Congratulations, you are already saving money and reducing your debt. To calculate how much, take the interest rate on your LOC and subtract the interest rate on your savings account. How much interest are you saving?

Repeat until you have cleared space or paid off the LOC in full.

Step 2: Attack Your Amortized Debt

Now, you will pick a dollar amount around 60 percent of your LOC or less that you will use to chunk down your amortized debt. You will make an extra "principal only" payment to the amortized debt from your LOC. You need to write this on the payment or check in the memo field. Now, repeat Step 1.

Step 3: Repeat

You have paid off your first chunk. Now, it is time to do it again. You repeat this process until you pay off that debt or whatever other target you had.

This is a real simple explanation of this strategy, but I know some people are visual learners and want to see an example.

Bonus: To watch a short twenty-minute video on how this works, go to thelaunchbuttonbook.com and log in. Click the "Strategy to Be Debt Free" button.

STUDENT EXAMPLES

I have seen this strategy help a lot of people save a lot of money and future interest payments. Most people do not really understand the power until after they are already in debt. Let me tell you the story of another student.

This student is an amazing individual who, when I first meet him, had a full-time job, four kids, a wife, was going to school to get his master's degree, and traveled around "on the side" as a gospel singer. You could say he was a busy man. His parents were hard-working immigrants who bought multifamily properties. As a kid, he was the handyman, property manager, etc. He wanted nothing to do with real estate for a long time. He joined my team and committed to becoming an entrepreneur and real estate investor. This is the first strategy that he applied. By simply reorganizing his debt, he saved over $26,000 in interest payments. He says, "Most people do not have enough pain in their life; that is why they will not change."

Would you like to keep $26,000 of your hard-earned money in your pocket instead of paying interest to a bank?

Another student who is also a military veteran was able to pay off a thirty-year mortgage on his rental property in three years. A husband-and-wife team who run an electrical contracting business were able to use one of their retirement accounts to chunk down their mortgage and save $47,000 in interest payments. I could go on and on with testimonials about this strategy.

Don't wait to schedule an appointment to talk with me or my team: hughzaretsky.com.

Let's see what we can do to help you keep more of your money and free up the cash flow to fund your business.

MORE NONTRADITIONAL FUNDING OPTIONS TO SET UP BEFORE YOU PRESS THE LAUNCH BUTTON!

Here are three of the more common options that you can establish before you leave your job. We have already discussed that once you leave your job, it is much harder to get a loan from a bank. These three funding options can provide a safety net in which you can get funding from anytime you want for anything you want. You do not need credit or income to get access to these options during your transition. You are legally lending your own money to yourself, and it is NOT taxable income, because it is a loan. The three options are: **Overfunded Whole Life Insurance**, **Self-Directed or Checkbook-Controlled Retirement Account**, and a **Health Savings Account (HSA)**.

Note: Now, I am not a financial advisor and each state has different laws, so I am just going to give you an overview of each of these options. You will want to meet with a financial advisor or specialist to go into the details of each option.

Overfunded Whole Life Insurance

I know a lot of people do not like whole life insurance and think it is a waste of money. They feel you should only do term insurance because it is cheaper. However, the top 1 percent (wealthy people) have been using this strategy for hundreds of years. Recently the US government figured out a way to cap "overfunding" whole life insurance. They created the Modified Endowment Contract (MEC) law, which caps the amount you can "overfund" on your whole life policy. This sounds like bad news, right? Well, the good news is that once your first policy is maxed out, you can get another life insurance policy to "overfund" and do it again.

The reason to establish a whole life policy does not have as much to do with the coverage or the death benefit. Those are both valuable and help with protecting you and your family in the future, as well as for legacy planning. My reason has to do with you being able to, in essence, "become your own bank." An overfunded life insurance account will give you access to capital during your policy period and beyond.

Full disclosure—I did not do this before I left the corporate world, either. I did not even know this strategy existed. I have paid over $30,000 in trainings to learn this wealth-building technique. The only thing I did before I left corporate was to buy a simple $100,000 life insurance policy that invests in the stock market. I bought it when I started working as a consultant at one of my very first jobs. I do not even remember really why I got it. Yes, I used it to fund one of my investments.

I am not a life insurance agent or financial advisor, so you will need to talk to one to get these policies set up for yourself and anyone else you want to protect. If you need a recommendation for an agent or a company, I would be happy to provide a list of companies that my students have used to get these set up.

Let's talk about some of the benefits an overfunded policy provides before we talk about what to look for in one.

Some Benefits of Overfunded Life Insurance

Potential Low-Interest-Rate Loans When You Need Them

What most people do not know is you can borrow up to 70–90 percent of the cash value of your life insurance to cover an emergency, expenses in your business, your personal life, or to invest in an opportunity. I have seen people use their loan to cover rehab expenses on a fix and flip, as a down payment on a property, to build out a video studio for their business, write a book, etc. If you have the right policy, your effective loan interest rate is also one of the lowest rates you can receive. The reason for the low interest rate is because you are still receiving dividends at the fixed interest (let's say 5 percent) on the full cash value, and then they charge you interest on the loan (let's say 7 percent), and your effective interest rate is only 2 percent. You usually can get the funds in seven to fifteen days after you request them.

Build a Large Safety Net with Low Premiums

With all life insurance, it is better to get a policy when you are younger. Most life insurance agents are trained to sell you the one with the largest death benefit to cover all of your and your family's needs. The problem with this is that a lot more of your payment goes toward the premium for the insurance and not the cash value of the policy. In my opinion, you want a policy with the minimum death benefit needed to cover your and your family's needs. This way, you can maximize the overfunded portion of the policy. The cash value will also increase your overall death benefit over time and might even grow the death benefit faster than a traditional whole life policy.

This strategy requires you to have financial discipline and overfund the policy each month or year, or it will not work. To become financially free, you need to think differently than the average person, and a traditional whole life policy is not what we are interested in.

Understand that life insurance agents get paid commissions and that is built into the premium of the policy. Typically, the higher the premium, the higher the commission. Life insurance agents being paid a commission is not a bad thing; you just need to understand their motivation. If an agent is willing to set up an overfunded policy without giving you a hard time, then you are probably working with a good agent. They are sacrificing their commissions but serving their customer's needs in a better way.

Let me give you an example with numbers. My first agent tried to sell me a whole life policy with a death benefit of about $750,000 and my premium payments would be $10,000 a year (based on age and health). Following the overfunding technique, I only got a $250,000 policy with a $2,500 annual premium instead (much more manageable in case things take a downward financial turn), but by "overfunding" it with a $10,000 a year payment, it will eventually provide over $1,000,000 in death benefits, and I will be able to access that overfunded amount at any time.

Do you see how you can get both benefits from this? These are just some of the things you learn about each week in our eFamily Ohana.

You Do Not Always Have to Overfund Your Policy

My premium on the $750,000 policy would have been $10,000 a year. Now, my premium is only $2,500, so if I have a financial hardship, I do not have to fund the "overfunded" portion. This gives me more flexibility.

Conservative Return to Balance Your Risk

In my opinion, you want a fixed guaranteed interest rate not tied to the stock market or another index. The worst thing would be for you to set up this policy as a safety net only to have the stock market crash when you need to take a loan from your policy. You would not be able to borrow as much money.

Since you are going to be taking a leap of faith into the entrepreneur and real estate investors world, there can be a high level of risk in your business or real estate. I personally feel you want your life insurance invested in the most conservative way possible to balance your risk.

Additional Riders Can Be Added to the Policy

There are some additional riders that you may want to add on to your policy, such as a convertible term policy or disablement rider. That is why you need to work with a good, qualified agent. If you need some recommendations, then join the eFramily (eFramily.com) platform to learn more on this strategy and how to find a good agent.

There is a lot more I could go into on this subject. There are certain advanced, wealth-building strategies available that allow you to leverage your spouse, children, or business partners to get cheaper whole life rates. This is enough to get you started. If you can get one of these "overfunding" policies set up for yourself before you leave your corporate job, you will be ahead of the game. If not, just do what you can to get this established as quickly as possible.

Self-Directed or Checkbook-Controlled Retirement Accounts

Most people are familiar with either a 401(k), 403B, TSP, etc. Most people do not know that you can create a "genuine" Self-Directed Retirement Account for your new business. A lot of traditional 401(k) plans will say they are "self-directed" because you get to pick from their stocks, bonds, Real Estate Investment Trusts (REITs), the mutual fund, etc. that they offer. When I say "genuine self-directed" this means you can buy property (houses, multifamily, commercial); invest in LLCs, S corps, tax deeds or liens; make private loans, etc., as well as the things a traditional 401(k) company offers.

This does put more financial responsibility on you to approve the deals and take ownership for your own financial decisions. In my opinion, I would rather be in control of my money. Again, you also have to be a grown-arse adult and get trained or work with top advisors to make these financial decisions. Warren Buffett listens to advisors, but he is the one who makes the final decisions and takes responsibility for the outcome.

Are you willing to be responsible for your financial future?

"Diversification is a protection against ignorance. It makes very little sense for those who know what they're doing."

—WARREN BUFFETT

If not, then leave your money with a financial planner and skip to the Generating Your Rocket Fuel exercise. If you are willing to accept full responsibility for your retirement plans, then keep reading.

I prefer Roth 401(k)s, posttax retirement savings accounts. Why? Because you get the benefits of both worlds as an entrepreneur. Your contributions have already been taxed before they enter your Roth account. You usually need to have some income in your business in order to fund any 401(k) plan, since traditional 401(k)s are pretax savings accounts.

There are two types of genuine self-directed retirement companies.

Third-Party Administrator Companies

The first type is very similar to traditional retirement accounts, where the genuine self-directed companies hold your money and you tell them what to invest in. For each transaction, you need to fill out a form, submit the required paperwork, etc. from that company's website. This is good for people who want to make the transition from corporate America and are just learning how to invest their own retirement money.

These companies either charge a monthly fee, a transaction fee, or an annual fee. However, they make sure that all transactions are arm-length transactions and that you do not violate any laws by touching your own retirement money. This is the safest option and least complicated method.

Checkbook-Controlled LLC Retirement Account

The other option is a checkbook-controlled LLC. This is more expensive to establish but you will not pay monthly or transaction fees. This is because you have the power to write a check for each investment and then deposit the money back into the LLC yourself. There is not a third-party administrator who approves each transaction.

You decide the investment, run the numbers, and then write the check. It is then on you to put the profits and initial investment back into the LLC when the investment is completed or profits are paid. You have 100 percent of the decision-making power and the speed to make investments.

The one potential issue is that you cannot touch your own money. If you do not dot the i's and cross the t's when you are doing your transactions, and you do touch your money, you will have to pay both taxes and penalties, anywhere from 20–40 percent. You no longer have retirement account protection for your investments. Therefore, you want to make sure you are educated on what to do and what not to do.

I suggest you only use checkbook-controlled retirement accounts if you have been fully trained on the rules and laws.

Using Your Genuine Self-Directed Retirement Account to Invest in Real Estate

One of the benefits of retirement accounts, 401(k)s, IRAs, etc., are **nonrecourse loans**. If you want your retirement account to invest in a property, and you cannot afford to buy the property with your retirement account money, you can get a nonrecourse loan. This loan requires a much higher-percentage down payment.

What does nonrecourse mean? It means the lender can only go after the asset that loan is based on. They cannot go after your retirement account or any other assets. In this case, it is a house or commercial building. This is why typically with nonrecourse loans you need to put in 20–50 percent of the investment as the down payment for the loan. In a worst-case scenario, where the lender has to foreclose and take back the property, they want to make sure there is enough equity in the deal to cover the expense of the potential foreclosure and filing fees.

Health Savings Account (HSA)

Health insurance is a big expense in today's world. You will want a plan for this before you leave your job. Did you know you can use your HSA to fund your business and real estate? Most people are familiar with health insurance and flextime policies that allow you to take money out pretax for health-related expenses, but at the end of the year, if you do not use the money, you lose it. With an HSA, if you do not use the money, you can keep it to invest in real estate or make loans.

HSA accounts can be funded with pretax dollars and can help you lower your monthly payment because they *only* work with high-deductible health insurance. (You will need to check with your insurance company and your state laws to see if this option is available to you.) HSAs act like retirement accounts, and you can use the funds to invest in equities, real estate, business, etc. That is one of the huge benefits of HSAs—they eventually convert into traditional retirement accounts.

The other benefit is with the right HSA investments, it can eventually become a self-funding account. You can invest your HSA funds into a rental property, and the income you receive from the property can pay your monthly health insurance premiums.

* * *

You are starting to see some innovative financial concepts, and you can see why we should have been taught this in school. To learn more innovative strategies, go to eFramily.com. But learning these financial and funding concepts is not enough. You actually have to go out there and apply them, so you can push the launch button on your business. You want access to as much capital as possible before you leave your job!

EXERCISE:
Generating Your Rocket Fuel!

Do you want your answers in a digital format? If so, go to thelaunchbuttonbook.com and click the login button to create your own The Launch Button Blueprint for Success PDF!

- **How are you going to fuel your new business?** Make a list of resources that you have to fuel your entrepreneur business.

  * Can you "bootstrap" (savings, cash, items to sell, etc.)?

  * Can you implement a creative finance strategy to fund your business? If so, which one?

  * Can you leverage your personal credit to fund your business?

  * Can you build and leverage business credit to fund your business?

  * Can you take on credit or money partners? If so, who would you consider and why?

* Can you leverage a hard money lender to fund your business?

• **Can you establish innovative funding solutions to fuel your business before you leave your job?**

* Can you set up and fund an Overfunded Whole Life Insurance policy?

* Can you set up and fund a Genuine Self-Directed or Checkbook-Controlled Retirement account?

* Can you set up a Health Savings Account (HSA)?

* Can you implement the interest reduction strategy and "chunking?"

• **How much fuel can you create from using the traditional and innovative strategies for your business?**

• **Is that enough to get you started?**

Bonus: Do you want a free funding assessment to see how much capital you can get? Well, log into thelaunchbuttonbook.com and click "The Free Funding Assessment" button.

LAUNCHING YOUR BUSINESS

STAGE 1

10

Preparing to Press the Launch Button!

Changing Your Habits to Support Your New Business

Changing Your Habits

It is time to start implementing some new habits to prepare for leaving the corporate world or your job.

YOU HAVE ALL HEARD THAT KNOWLEDGE IS POWER. WELL, I DO not believe that because there are lots of people much smarter than me who still work a nine-to-five job. They are building someone else's dream instead of their own. It is not about knowledge; it is **applied knowledge** that is power. That is why I have created exercises in this book for you to start implementing (and applying) the knowledge I am sharing with you.

The only difference between you and me is time and applied knowledge. You have already heard my story earlier about working the 50x40x40. I do not care if you are a high school dropout or have your MBA, PhD, JD, etc. I have helped people with all levels of education launch their business and fire their boss. The real question is: are you ready to go to work building your dream life instead of someone else's?

> *"The graveyard is the richest place on earth because it is there that you will find all the hopes and dreams that were never fulfilled."*

—LES BROWN

Most people are not willing to take consistent daily action to make their hopes and dreams come true, and their amazing ideas end up in the graveyard.

Are you ready to start taking action so you can make your goals/dreams a reality?

Bonus: If you are, then go to thelaunchbuttonbook.com and log in. Click "I am ready to take action," and we will send you an invite to a private Facebook Group of action-takers.

The goal with the FB group is to post six days a week with the action steps you are taking that day. It does not matter what time you post each day. You just have to do it before you go to bed to hold yourself accountable.

WASTED TIME MAKING DECISIONS OR REMAKING DECISIONS

I have designed a few systems to help you further define your goals and track your productivity. I have tested these systems and refined them over time based on my own research and working with my nationwide team of entrepreneurs and real estate investors. One of the reasons these systems are so successful is they can help you make good decisions each day. Implementing these strategies will give you back thirty minutes to two hours each day.

Most of us only have a certain number of good decisions we get to make each day. That is why most people cheat on their diet late at night or end up just watching TV instead of being productive. They ran out of good decisions. There is a reason why some top entrepreneurs like Steve Jobs and Mark Zuckerberg all wear the same outfit each day. They do not waste a good decision on choosing their outfit.

What most people do not realize is that they waste a significant amount of time making decisions. How much time do you spend each day fighting to figure out what you should do next?

Some people say, "I do not waste time because I have a to-do list, Hugh!" It still takes you up to thirty minutes to figure out which tasks on your to-do list to do next. If you do not have a copy of your to-do list next to you, then it takes *even longer* to decide.

Have you ever gone through a day and forgotten to do something major for your job or family?

If so, then you let life, or the universe, control your day. You can stop this by winning your morning, getting your three big tasks done each day, and protecting your schedule. Most people overestimate what they can do in a day but underestimate what they can do in a week. This puts you on track to make your goals and dreams come true. I will explain each of these theories and habits in more detail below, but if you need additional help, go to hughzaretsky.com and click on books, or go to Amazon and search for *"The Steps to Fire Your Boss - 5 Week Productivity Journal"* or "Hugh Zaretsky" to order it. Installing these three principles/habits will help you get laser focused and take control of your day, week, month, etc.

ESTABLISHING AN EFFECTIVE MORNING ROUTINE

When you launch your career or dream life, you have to build new habits for everything you do, including your morning routine.

The easiest way to make the transition is to start building these habits while you still have a job. You have a start time each day at work. When your boss and coworkers know your start time as well, it creates social pressure to get to work on time. If you consistently show up late, you might get fired or lose income, right? When you work for yourself, these social pressures go away. You must hold yourself accountable. It is important for you to create new morning routine habits.

Let's look at what you currently do before you commute to work. How do you get your day started? Write down all of the things you currently do from getting out of bed until leaving your home for work. Is it often stressful trying to get everything done and leave on time to get to work?

Next, let's look at your commute. Do you drive, take mass transit, bike, or walk to work? What do you do while you commute to work? Do you listen to music, books, trainings, podcasts, etc. to work on your mindset, gain knowledge, or just de-stress? Do you catch up on sleep during your commute on mass transit? Write down what you do. Look at your list. Are you maximizing and winning your morning or just getting by?

The first thing you will need to establish is your new morning routine. As you start to change it, your brain is going to freak out until your routine becomes your "new normal." There are a few major concepts that help you win your morning. They are gratitude, exercise or move, meditate or pray, knowledge or intelligence, nutrition, and your "big three," or as I call it, "get excited, make it happen, now—three times!"

GET EXCITED MAKE IT HAPPEN NOW - 3 TIMES

Your NEW Morning Routine

Do you want to set yourself up for a successful day? The best way to do this is to start your day the right way. You want your mind and body functioning at their highest levels to fight off stress and whatever the world or universe throws at you.

GRATITUDE

When you start your day with an attitude of gratitude, you raise your vibration and appreciation for the world. What three things are you thankful for today?

EXERCISE OR MOVE

Your 3,000-year-old brain is most fearful in the morning. By moving or exercising, you automatically change the chemicals in your brain and body, which puts you in a better mindset.

MEDITATE OR PRAY

It is time to ground yourself and meditate or pray to clear your brain. This way you can focus on your day and your goals!

INTELLIGENCE

Feed your brain something to help you in life or business. Keep a positive mindset, and learn something new. This builds your confidence and knowledge base.

NUTRITION

Feed your body the right food, water, and sleep to keep it functioning at a high level. You can choose to track the number of meals or what you eat, the amount of water you drink each day, and the number of hours you sleep each night.

3 BIG TASKS

We overestimate what we can do in a day and underestimate what we can do in a week! Write down your 3 Big Tasks of the day. Try to do them before lunch. When you get them done, then you have won your day!

WIN YOUR MORNING!

You have heard the saying "Win your morning, win your day!" Well, it is true! Completing your morning routine allows you to build confidence in yourself and prepares your mind and body for whatever life, the world, or the universe throws at you. This will reduce the stress in your life and allow you to live a healthier and more fulfilled life!

Join the eFramily to learn more at www.eframily.com

- **Gratitude:** What are you thankful for today? Most
  people focus on what they do not have, instead of focus-
  ing on things they are thankful for. You could be thankful for waking up, having electricity, family, friends,
  loved ones, etc. It can be small or big. When you start
  your day this way, you raise your energy, your vibration,
  and your appreciation for everything in the world.

- **Exercise or move:** Science has shown that our
  two-thousand-year-old brain has the highest level of
  the fear hormone, cortisol, when we first wake up in
  the morning. That is why the first thing we should do
  in the morning is jump out of bed and get moving. This
  automatically changes the hormones/chemicals in our
  body and reduces our cortisol levels while producing
  endorphins that put us in a good mood. This could be
  as simple as going for a walk, doing yoga, working out,
  or going on a strenuous run.

- **Meditation or prayer:** Now that you are in a good
  mood, it is easier to ground yourself without your
  brain worrying about the things you need to do or get
  done today. This allows you to pray or meditate in a
  more peaceful state.

- **Intelligence or knowledge:** Now you are in the right
  mindset and ready to feed your brain some knowledge. This could be something you want to learn or
  something to strengthen your mindset. There are so
  many options in today's world, from reading a book to
  listening to an Audible book or podcast, or watching a
  YouTube video.

- **Health and nutrition:** In order to have a big impact, you need to live a long life, so taking care of your nutrition, hydrating, and getting enough sleep are very important. There are many things you can track each day: intermittent fasting, number of meals, calorie intake, the amount of water you drink and/or hours you sleep. We all function better when we have six to eight hours of sleep, drink enough water, and eat a clean diet. You choose what you want to track and there are plenty of apps to help you track this information.

- **Your three big tasks for the day:** Each morning, you identify your three big tasks that you want to accomplish that day. I know three big tasks in a day does not sound like a lot, but that is ninety big tasks in a month and 1,095 in a year. They can be business, personal, or a combination of things. For most people, the easiest time to complete these tasks is in the morning when their willpower is the strongest. However, you do not get to go to bed until you have accomplished these three *big* tasks. Deal?

Most people also find they have more clarity in the morning before they eat because digesting food takes a significant amount of energy and resources from the body. By following this routine and winning your morning, you will take control of your day and set yourself up for success.

Just go to hughzaretsky.com and click on books or go to Amazon and search for *"The Steps to Fire Your Boss - 5 Week Productivity Journal"* or "Hugh Zaretsky" to order it.

If you do not define and stick to your new morning routine, then you may create some bad habits working from home, such as:

- **Not showering until the afternoon:** When you only commute from your bed to your couch, there is no one saying you need to be on time or look good. Sometimes people feel themselves diving into work after their morning routine and then comes the afternoon and they realize they haven't showered or eaten.

- **Distracted by errands or "honey-do" lists:** Some people, when they are working from home, get distracted by errands like laundry, food shopping, babysitting, "honey-do" lists (list of tasks or chores from a spouse or family member), etc.

- **Distracted by TV:** Some people try to work with the TV on at home. Do you do this at your job? No. It should be obvious that when you work from home, you cannot have the TV on while you are working.

- **Distracted by food:** Since you are working at home, some people get bored, nervous, etc., and go to the fridge to get a drink or a snack. Some people get into bad habits because the fridge is so close. Therefore, it is important that you not keep a lot of sugary snacks around.

- **Kids:** Having young kids at home can be a big distraction, even if you have a babysitter. The kids know you are in your office, and if they want attention, they might bang on the door or start crying. It is important for your business that you stay focused on what you want to accomplish during business hours.

- **Distracted by family and friends:** If there are other people in your home like family or friends, they can distract you by trying to include you or get you to do things with them instead of your work.

- **Taking on more family responsibility:** One thing I see that tends to bring down entrepreneurs once they fire their boss is that they take on more family responsibilities because they no longer must go to a traditional job. Therefore, some family or friends may feel that you now have more "free time." For example, picking the kids up from school, taking them to school, babysitting, taking care of a parent or loved one, etc. There is no real harm to this, as long as you adjust your schedule to accommodate this change and continue to put in the required number of business hours.

  * This can become a problem when people just cut back their efforts in their business to take care of these additional responsibilities and do not put the time back into their business. Your business then begins to suffer and generates less income, which adds more stress to your life. This, in turn, causes more stress with your financial budget and eventually with your family. This is a slippery slope that could lead to a downward spiral and all the way back to a nine-to-five job.

Creating a plan for your morning routine will help your day get off to a good start by preparing your mind and body to be productive. This will automatically build confidence in yourself. It will make it easier for you to do your big three tasks of the day and build your business. All because you won your morning.

BIG ROCK THEORY

It is important to prioritize your three big tasks for the day, because often we do not want to do them. It is usually out of fear that we tend to procrastinate and avoid them. However, once we get our big tasks done, the rest of the day becomes easier, and you have more confidence. This is part of the success cycle.

Taking Action → Builds Confidence →
Creates Results → Leads to Success

If you complete all three tasks, you have had a successful day. Congratulations!

This is exactly what the big rock theory is about. It categorizes tasks as sand, pebbles, and big rocks. Most people start their day doing the easy, small tasks represented by the "sand." Unfortunately, most people leave their big tasks for the end of the day when their willpower is weak and they are tired. This leads to tasks being pushed off to the next day or not fitting in the jar. The only way everything fits in the jar is to start with the big rocks or your big tasks. You then add the pebbles (medium tasks). Finally, you add the sand and it fills in all of the crevices and the jar is full.

You can track your morning routine and your big tasks on a piece of paper, on a spreadsheet, on your phone, or you can use my productivity journal to help keep you on track. By setting these tasks up the night before or during your morning routine, you will get back ten minutes to three hours of your day.

As you start to use the productivity journals or your new morning routine, your brain is going to start playing tricks on you. I need you to recognize this fear or trick your brain is playing. Just push through and continue to use the journals or tracking systems. After a few weeks, you will see that this fear either goes away or stops because you have tricked your brain into a habit. This new system and habit have become your "new normal," and your brain is now used to them. In fact, it gets to the point where if you stop using them, your brain will freak out and push you to get back on track.

As I mentioned earlier, it is applied knowledge that is powerful. How are you going to start applying this to your life today?

Remember the fortune is made behind closed doors in your mind during after-work hours (either between five and nine in the morning or between eight at night and two in the morning). What change are you going to apply today? What will you do today to build your business?

If you treat your business like a business, it will pay you like a business. If you treat it like a hobby, it will cost you like a hobby.

WHERE ARE YOU GOING TO RUN YOUR BUSINESS FROM?

Some people are *not* able to work from home and that is perfectly OK. A lot of people got a taste of working from home during our COVID quarantine. I coached many of my corporate and teacher friends on ways to work effectively from home. Nowadays, there are office spaces, Starbucks, and restaurants with free Wi-Fi available around the world. You can work from one of these locations or be in a coworking space around other professionals. Sometimes just being around other professionals is all someone needs to be productive.

Look into Shared Offices or Memberships

It is OK if you start out working from home and realize it is not right for you. Some people can handle the "monotony" of working from home and not interacting with other people. How did you do during the COVID quarantine? Were you productive?

If you are not good at working from home, then you need to investigate some alternatives, which I shall cover in this section. I will be the first one to admit I was not good working from home for many years. It was not until the coronavirus quarantine when I finally felt OK with it. That is roughly fifteen years after firing my boss. I originally tried working from home and realized it did not work for me. I need the social interaction of being around other businesspeople. When I began looking for coworking spaces back in 2006, there were only a few big-name companies offering these services. Nowadays, there are all types of coworking spaces. Some are dedicated towards a certain industry or theme. You just need to find a solution that matches your needs or budget.

As an entrepreneur, it can be lonely working during the day with no one to talk to or be around. This is sometimes how stay-at-home parents feel. When their significant other gets home, they just want to talk to another adult. At a shared office space, you are surrounded by other entrepreneurs. They may or may not be in the same industry as you, but they face similar challenges, and you may have a lot in common with them. Coworking spaces can become like incubators. Collaboration and relationships are built in coworking spaces. That is an added benefit for entrepreneurs. Just make sure you build this cost into your budget as you prepare to launch your business.

If you are good working from home, you may want to research these types of places and potentially get a monthly membership. That way, if you have an important meeting, you can meet in a professional conference room or office instead of in your home. Memberships at some of the larger shared office spaces will allow you to access affiliate offices in other cities or countries.

This can also help you when you travel or if you eventually want to become a nomad entrepreneur.

A nomad entrepreneur is someone who can work from anywhere in the world. They travel whenever and wherever they want. It is not all Jet Skis, traveling, and fun. You still need to generate income. Now, you do not have to go full **digital nomad**. Digital nomads are people who use telecommunications technologies to earn a living and conduct their life in a nomadic manner. However, many people want to be "snowbirds," "bicoastal," or work from different places. One thing to consider when you are looking at shared office space or memberships is to see if they have locations in different cities, states, or countries.

TESTING YOUR BUSINESS IN A COWORKING SPACE VERSUS GOING STRAIGHT TO A PRIVATE OFFICE

I personally believe most entrepreneurs should transition into a coworking space before getting their own private office. There are a couple different reasons for this belief.

1. **Coworking offers month-to-month leases vs. your own office, which will typically require annual leases of one year or more.** The nice thing about most shared spaces is that you sign a month-to-month lease and are not locked into a long-term lease. You do typically need to give a one-month security deposit, as well. This helps to not only give you flexibility but also reduces your cost. If you were to open your own office, you may be locked into a yearlong lease or

multiple-year lease. As a new business, you may be
required to pay one to three months' security deposit
as well.

2. **Coworking spaces typically come built out vs.
   your own office, for which you will most likely be
   responsible for the cost of a buildout.** Coworking
   spaces are designed for entrepreneurs to be able to
   grow within them starting with hot desks (a single
   workspace used by several coworkers during different time periods) and eventually to dedicated private
   offices. They usually come prebuilt and you just select
   the right hot desk, private space, or office that matches
   your needs. You will not have the initial construction
   costs of building out your space and putting up or
   taking down walls, doors, etc. If you rent your own
   traditional office space for your business, then you may
   have the additional construction cost to convert the
   space to meet your needs.

3. **Coworking spaces have prebuilt infrastructure
   vs. building out your own infrastructure in your
   own office.** When I say infrastructure, this includes
   internet access (both hardwired and wireless), phone
   systems and support, running network cables or putting
   in wireless routers, printers, copiers, etc. This might
   also include coffee, tea, water machines, and more. Each
   one of these has a cost to buy and install. However, in a
   coworking space, these are already included and paid
   for. If you were to build out your own office, then you
   would need to get quotes and add these costs to the

budget for your own private office. You must consider the cost of buying or leasing printers, copiers, etc.

4. **Coworking spaces usually come furnished vs. you furnishing your own office.** Coworking spaces are usually prefurnished with desks, filing cabinets, chairs, etc. If you build out your own office, then you will either have to purchase or lease your own furniture. Some people do like this better, but it is a question of the cost and how fast your business will grow.

In my opinion, this initial up-front cost is not worthwhile when you are trying to grow and expand your business. Now, there are always exceptions to this rule. For example, one business I run needs a fifty- to sixty-person conference room once a week and there are not many such options near where this business operates. It was cheaper to get our own office than to rent out conference space monthly. However, even this business started out in a shared space. We only needed conference room space for fifteen to thirty people. We got our own office only when we had grown enough to justify the cost.

I remember a funny story of a guy who bought a membership to one of the airline's private clubs at the airport. He made that his coworking space and commuted to the airport each day. It was cheaper than getting an office, and the club served free snacks, coffee, tea, etc. It was also a professional space that had free internet, private cubicles, conference rooms, and even showers he could use. I believe the airlines have since closed that loophole. However, it gives you an idea of what some entrepreneurs will do to find the right office space.

WHAT SHOULD YOU CONSIDER WHEN LOOKING AT A COWORKING SPACE?

Typically, coworking spaces have membership levels based on need. What type of usage do you need?

- **Basic-level membership/hot desk or spot:** This is the lowest form of entry to most shared office spaces. You typically pay a monthly membership fee. Think of it like a gym membership. It usually gives you the ability to come in and use the common areas (no dedicated space) when needed. This shared space may be desks, tables, couches, booths, etc. It is usually first come, first served.

- **A dedicated desk:** You actually have a desk or a dedicated spot that is yours that you use each day. It could be in an open room but typically comes with a lockable filing cabinet or drawer to keep your belongings in. It should include a dedicated phone with voicemail, plus a certain number of printouts or copies per month. You should also receive more conference room credits than the basic monthly membership.

- **A private office:** As your business grows, you may need or want more privacy. These private offices can usually hold one to four people. This is also important if you are dealing with private/confidential information. Most of the offices come prefurnished so you do not have the cost of buying furniture. You should have full support from a receptionist, mail services, and parking, and you can bring in your own copier/printer or get additional copies.

Note: These are typical membership levels, but you will need to ask some common-sense questions as you look at space.

Coworking spaces give you the ability to scale quickly without having to invest a lot of capital into a build-out infrastructure, office furniture, etc. They also give you flexibility for rapid business growth or a decline. You are not locked into a long-term lease. After you have consistent monthly and yearly income and can predict the growth of your business, I advise looking into getting your own office space.

EXERCISE:
Some Things to Consider as You Create Your New Morning Routine ("Get Excited, Make It Happen, Now—Three Times!")

Do you want your answers in a digital format? If so, go to thelaunchbuttonbook.com and click the login button to create your own The Launch Button Blueprint for Success PDF!

- What are three things you are grateful for each day?

- How are you going to ground yourself (meditate, pray, etc.) each day?

- When are you going to develop your knowledge or intelligence (read, journal, listen to podcasts, etc.)?

- How can you improve your healthy eating, sleeping, and hydration routines?

- What are your big three tasks for the day?

- How much time is your new morning routine going to take?

- Determine whether you are still going to get up at the same time, earlier, or later.

- When can you fit everything into your new morning routine?

- What activity did you do on your commute to work that you need to recreate?

- What is the start date for your new morning routine?

Bonus: If you need more help, then go to hughzaretsky. com and click on books or go to Amazon and search for *"The Steps to Fire Your Boss—5 Week Productivity Journal"* or "Hugh Zaretsky" to order it.

Questions to Ask for Coworking Spaces

Here are general questions to ask to see if the space matches your needs:

- During which hours is the space open?

- Do they offer weekend hours?

- What are their membership levels (basic, hot desk, dedicated desk, private office, etc.)?

- Does it include a mailbox, or can you have mail delivered to the office?

- Do you get credits or a certain number of conference room hours each month?

- Do larger conference rooms require more credits or hours to reserve?

- Can you buy more conference room credits or hours? What is the additional cost per credit or hour each month?

- Is this their only location or can you get access to multiple locations? Is there an additional cost for this?

- Are you able to print a certain number of documents or make copies each month? How much is each additional printout or copy in black and white and/ or color?

- Do you get a phone number?

- Will the receptionist answer your phone and forward calls to your cell phone?

- If not, is there an additional fee for this service?

- Is there free parking, or do you have to pay for parking?

- Can your guests, clients, or coworkers park for free as well?

- Do you have access to a kitchen in the space?

- Do they offer coffee, tea, water, or other items for free?

- Do they have networking events for members or offer other special events?

- What other amenities or services are included with your monthly fee?

Remember, this is not an all-inclusive list. You will need to use some common sense in considering other questions. I also highly recommend asking questions about a dedicated desk and a private office because your goal is to grow your business.

11

Launch Your Dream Business or Passion

Leverage Your Assets,
Increase Your Cash Flow and Momentum

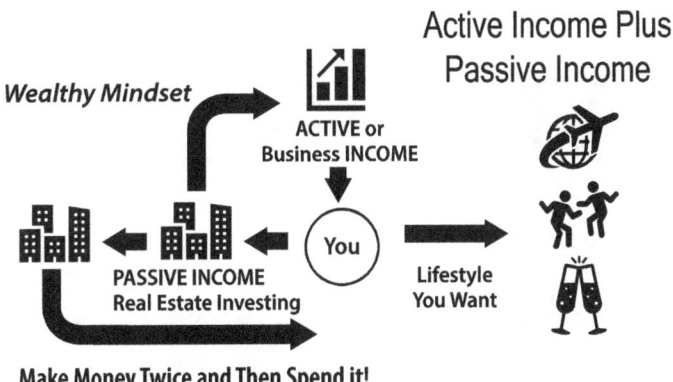

Leverage the assets you already have and turn them into income streams. You can turn anything you enjoy into an income stream.

AT THIS POINT, YOU HAVE ALREADY STARTED PAYING YOURSELF first and establishing your rocket fuel (a.k.a. funding options). You have also created your business plan and SWOT analysis, and identified your goals. Now it is time to launch your side hustle, if you haven't already started generating income from it. You want to see if your idea has potential. We will also work on switching more of your expenses to your business and increasing your tax deductions to free up additional cash flow. More cash flow equals more fuel for your rocket ship. Now push the launch button! We have ignition!

What assets do you have to leverage as a bridge to your ultimate plan? We need to identify some assets that you already have so you can leverage or test your business vision.

- Time

- Passion

- Knowledge

- Relationships

- Money

- Financial assets

- Your business

- Other assets

Let's talk about the assets you have and how you can leverage those while you are taking your first steps towards making your dreams come true. We have already talked about finding your passion and leveraging your financial assets. Let's talk about some of the other assets you have.

TIME

Create hours each day that you are going to work on your business or side hustle. This is important. Remember, consistent, daily action done over time has a compounding effect. What are the hours each day that you are going to work your business?

KNOWLEDGE

Do you need to gain additional knowledge?

Look at your SWOT analysis. Is there an area that you can convert from a weakness to a strength? For me, I needed to gain more knowledge in a field that I did not know anything about. That is why I signed up for the speaker's boot camp training. I wanted to quickly learn how to give effective presentations and raise capital. I could have spent hours, days, weeks, and months researching the information on the internet or YouTube. Or, I could pay for the training and learn from experts all in one place in three days. I was willing to invest in myself, so I could push the launch button, fire my boss, and get more free time.

If you do not have extra income, you can take an internship or volunteer to get the information needed, rather than paying for training. You can leverage your free time to get the training you need. You can often find these volunteer opportunities via relationships or from referrals. They are a great way to learn new skills.

RELATIONSHIPS

I wanted to continue to improve my speaking skills after the initial boot camp. Since I had stayed in contact with my speaker-trainer, he invited me back to the trainings. I would help him evaluate the new people's presentations. The company saved money by only having to pay for one speaker's fee and travel instead of two. My friend (the trainer) got to keep a larger share of the commissions, and I got a free refresher. The students got a second evaluation from someone who had been in their shoes as a new speaker. It definitely was a win–win–win.

Depending on where you live, you may need to travel to attend live trainings or do them on a webinar. During our COVID stay at home, online meetings have become acceptable, but it is still harder to build relationships over a webinar than in person. During breaks, lunch, and evenings is where the relationships are formed. This is why I highly recommend traveling for trainings, to be able to meet people in person. There is also the potential tax deduction I will explain later in this chapter.

START YOUR BUSINESS AS A SIDE HUSTLE

Starting a side hustle or your business is easy to do with the new shared economy. It used to be very expensive, but technology and sites like Uber, Lyft, Task Rabbit, Door Dash, Fiverr,

Upwork, Amazon, Airbnb, and VRBO have greatly reduced your up-front costs. There are more sites popping up every day and one will match your passion. You get to leverage their websites, databases, and marketing/advertising to see if your business idea will make it before you have a lot of expenses. You will need to check the laws in your area first, of course. Which site matches your business idea or passion? For me, it was Airbnb.

Airbnb Became My Side Hustle

I was introduced to Airbnb through a friend back in 2013. My friend approached me about renting my condo out on a website while I traveled. He said, "When you travel for your events, I will clean your apartment for free and give you a check when you get back. Does that work?"

I told him he had me at "clean your apartment for free." I truly would have been happy with just that. This started my Airbnb experience before most people knew what Airbnb was or how it worked. I am grateful for that introduction. My unit helped prove several theories that my businesses still use today. In fact, I have incorporated these theories into my Airbnb training program that I teach to help people to maximize their revenue.

Note: The Airbnb/vacation rentals/nightly rentals/short-term rentals strategy is still so *new*, it will be your responsibility to stay informed on the laws and regulations in the country, state, county, township, HOA, POA, etc.

Depending on the city, state, and area you live in, you can rent your whole place, part of a place, a bedroom, etc. on Airbnb. The research you do on the ever-changing laws will determine the legal way to do it. This side hustle income can be very profitable, because it does not take a lot of time to set up, especially if you already own your property or acquire an investment property. This is how some people are living for free in their homes. They are getting their mortgage(s), property owner association (POA)/homeowners association (HOA) fees, insurance, and taxes paid for. Plus, there are some additional profits for renting them on Airbnb. They have truly turned their home into an asset.

If you rent and/or are going to use the lease and re-lease policy, then I highly recommend you have a conversation with your landlord first before you start implementing this strategy. After your landlord approves your request, you have the same opportunities as mentioned above for owning a property. I have trained many students with this strategy and taught them how they can save a significant amount of money by acquiring these cash cow types of properties. Sometimes we buy them, and sometimes we just lease them. This is just one of the many theories we're proving with my unit. This started a unique journey for me that continues to grow and expand with the new shared economy.

DID YOU KNOW YOU CAN MAKE MONEY ON AIRBNB WITHOUT A PROPERTY?

There is a new way to make money on Airbnb and some other sites that no one is really talking about yet. People book properties on Airbnb to stay in a city like a local, and now anyone can create a "local experience" on the site. You do not need to own a property to post an experience. You just need to have a passion or a business in that city. Even the random facts and stuff you have gathered in your brain about your city or town can now be used to generate income for you.

One way to get ideas or to see if your business will work is to search on Airbnb or any of the sites mentioned above to find similar experiences or listings to what you want to create. This will give you an idea of the details/length of the experience and the price that you can eventually charge for your experience or business. If this is your passion or long-term business idea, then Airbnb just made it cheap and easy to launch your idea. You do not need to spend a lot of money on marketing, advertising, or building a website. Look at the sites mentioned above to see if your idea fits. There are always new sites popping up, so you can also search on Google.

Does your idea fit into one of the current categories on Airbnb? Here are just some of the categories on the site:

- Workshops

- Crafts, cooking, music, fashion, art, surf, wellness, business classes

- Bar crawl

- Culture, history, or food walk

- Kayaking

- Animal encounter

- Coffee tasting

- Social gathering

- Fishing

- Magic show

- Boat ride

- Photo shoot

- Dinner party

There are many different experiences you can create on Airbnb. If your idea does not fit into any of the categories, check the other sites I mentioned or do a Google search for the appropriate site for your business.

Once you find the right site, there are a few critical elements to get your business or experience seen:

- **A great cover photo:** There will be several similar experiences or businesses on the site, so you want yours to jump off the page.

- **A catchy headline for your experience:** Use keywords to advertise your unique perspective. This will cause your business to pop up in more searches. This is exactly what we do with Airbnb or short-term, rental-stay listings.

- **Get five-star reviews fast:** Get positive five-star reviews as quickly as possible. This may require dropping your price in the beginning to get more bookings and reviews. Once you get five-star reviews, the algorithms of the site will include your listing in more searches. This should allow you to then raise your price(s).

These three things will help you turn your side hustle into an income-generating activity without having to spend a lot of money on marketing and advertising. They also give you the ability to add upsells for your business. You are able to build a customer base from these sites. You can then invest in more traditional marketing and sales channels to promote your business because you have already tested it. You already know it works and will fill a need.

REDUCING YOUR TAXABLE INCOME

Once you have picked your site and created your listing, you are in business. Technically, your business needs to generate one dollar in the first year to get all of the tax deductions listed below. You should consult with a CPA to determine if you should be doing business as a **Doing Business As** (DBA) or form an LLC or S corp.

You now have a legitimate business that will be generating income. This means you qualify to get access to over three hundred business tax deductions. There is not a different tax law for the wealthy and the poor. There is only one. The wealthy just hire people who have read the law and understand it. The poor and middle-class pay their neighbor, go to H&R Block, etc. The crazy thing is the fee you pay your neighbor or CPA to do your taxes is *also* tax-deductible. If your neighbor can get you a $2,000 refund by paying the $250 to do your taxes, a CPA who understands business taxes can probably get you a $6,000-plus refund. It'll cost you $1,500, but you still come out ahead! Plus, the next year you would get to write off the $1,500 fee. It is a win–win–win.

> **Note:** Remember, tax laws change every year, so talk with your CPA in advance to see what they can do for you. Not all CPAs are the same and some specialize in different areas. I am not a CPA or attorney, so I can only tell you what I do. It is up to you to verify with your CPA and/or attorney.

TAX EXAMPLES

Let's talk about some of these three-hundred-plus tax deductions. I have already mentioned a few throughout this book, but here are a few more to get you started.

Technology Is Always Changing

Stop paying for new or upgraded cell phones, laptops, smartwatches, etc. with after-tax dollars. Move them over to your business expenses. You need upgraded technology to keep pace with your competition and to keep your business running.

Meals and Entertainment

You can still deduct meals but not entertainment for your business meetings. As long as you can show that you have talked about your business in some way with the other person, then you can write off 50 percent of your meal. Go out and be more social to spread the word. Get feedback on your business, and you can reduce your taxable income at the same time.

You will need supporting documentation to pass an IRS audit. You can keep the physical receipt or take a picture of the receipt. The IRS would like to see five things on a receipt. They are:

1. A date and time.

2. Restaurant name and address.

3. Total of the bill with tip.

And written on the back of the receipt:

1. Who was there?

2. What did you talk about during the meal?

This is what the IRS requires to pass an audit. If you drive to the meeting, then you would also need to track mileage and/or expenses for transportation to and from the meeting as well, if it is not part of your normal commute.

Business-Related Trainings
and Travel

What about traveling to attend trainings to learn new skills and to gain more knowledge for your business? In my opinion, the easiest and fastest way to gain knowledge is to attend a live training or boot camp. Unfortunately, most people blow off or do not value the training they get for free. Actually paying for higher-level training seems to get people to focus and pay attention. If you travel for a business training and more than 50 percent of the entire trip is business-related, then of course, your trip and meals would be tax deductible. When I travel, I always plan a little extra fun time. If you want to be more conservative, then according to most CPAs, anything that happens twenty-four hours before or after a meeting is automatically tax deductible. I am not a CPA, so double-check with your CPA before booking your travel, and they will give you the guidelines. These same tax deductions also apply if you need to travel for a meeting with a client or customer, or for your board meeting, leadership conference, sales retreat, etc. Yes, you must document these meetings, but who cares. This will help you plan your business trips and some fun in the most effective manner.

All you need is a day planner or cell phone calendar to track all your meetings, meals, mileage, etc. Most people put this information into a spreadsheet or bookkeeping software like Quick-Books. Put down *all* of your business-related expenses, meals, and meetings in your calendar.

Augusta Tax Break

Believe it or not, you can rent your own home out for up to fourteen days, and all of the income you receive is tax-free. This strategy will work on your primary home or second home. It will not work on investment property or short-term Airbnb property. Once you rent it out for the fifteenth day, you must pay tax on all the income.

This is Section 280A(g) of the Internal Revenue Code and is often called "The Augusta Rule." The plain language of this section states that a taxpayer can: (a) rent out his or her residence to someone else, including a corporation; (b) for fourteen days or less during a calendar year; and (c) not report the income received from the rental(s). To follow the logic to its ultimate tax conclusion, if the income is not includable in gross income, taxes are not owed on that income.

The Augusta Rule got its name from the Masters golf tournament in Augusta, Georgia. There are not a lot of hotels near the golf course. Instead of staying in a hotel farther away, the professional golfers would rather rent out a nice home on or near the golf course. The homeowners were able to get a tax loophole pushed through, so they would not have to pay any tax on the income. There is only one tax code to remember, which means you get to use the same loophole for your own home or second home.

* * *

You now have opened your own business and are required to have an annual meeting to review bylaws, etc. Most big businesses will rent out a hotel boardroom or conference center for their annual meeting and pay reasonable rent to the hotel for the meeting. The Augusta Rule instead allows you to rent your home to your business instead of paying for a hotel. You will need to charge your business a "reasonable rate," so check with your CPA to determine what that is. Then document those rates and hold on to them in case you get audited.

The benefits of doing this are:

1. It reduces your business income by the rental amount as a normal business deduction. (Talk to your CPA about how to do this.)

2. You do not have to pay taxes on this rental income.

Let's do an example with numbers. If $1,500 is a reasonable cost per day for a meeting room and hotel rooms for each of your corporate board members, then this means you would charge your business $21,000 for the fourteen days (TradersLog.com

Research 2021). You just reduced your business income by $21,000 and put $21,000 in your pocket tax-free.

If you really want to maximize your tax deductions, it is important to talk with your CPA in September or October to start tax planning for your year-end to get the largest refund. They can take a look at your financial situation and give you ideas and thoughts on how to save/reduce the amount of money you would potentially owe on your taxes. If you wait until after the calendar year ends, CPAs are limited by the things that they can deduct. There are many more tax deductions we could talk about, but more advanced strategies should be taught by a CPA or attorney.

Do you see how you can shift these expenses from your personal life to your business? This reduces your taxable income, and you get to keep more of your paycheck. Are the blinders coming off now?

RIDE THE WAVE OF MOMENTUM

Whenever you start your business, you want to make sure you ride the wave of momentum and keep moving forward. A lot of people do not understand that in the early stages of any business, you need to ride the wave of momentum and push extra hard. Momentum can help with that push and take your business to new heights. I see most entrepreneurs sit back after they have completed their first real estate deal or business success. Instead, this is when they should double their efforts and use that success to notify everyone who might be interested in their services.

Ride the Wave of *Momentum*

"The most powerful ingredient in business is positive momentum. Get it and keep it."

—UNKNOWN

I also see people break their momentum when they set a goal and reach it. *This is not the time to take a break.* This is actually the time to double down their energy and efforts. They are pumped up about their success for hitting XYZ and that energy flows out of them. New business ideas or real estate deals will be attracted to you because of your success. Ride this wave as long as you can, because it will eventually slow down. That is when you take the break and give yourself the reward.

EXERCISE:
Assets You Can Leverage and Tax-Reduction Strategies

Do you want your answers in a digital format? If so, go to thelaunchbuttonbook.com and log in to create your own The Launch Button Blueprint for Success PDF!

- Which assets can you leverage?

    * Time

    * Passion

    * Knowledge

    * Relationships

    * Money

    * Financial Assets

    * Your Business

    * Other Assets

- Determine if your business idea fits into one of the side hustles or Airbnb experiences. Can you use them to fund your business? If not, what other site does it fit into?

  * If it fits into a site, then create a plan to start working your side hustle to fund your business.

- Which tax-reduction strategies can you implement in your business? If you do not see one, then contact a CPA to learn more tax-reduction strategies.

- Schedule a meeting with a CPA to discuss the best structure for your business and associated costs.

12

Build a System for Your Business and Future Life

Build a System to Automate Your Business

How can you start to outsource or make your business not location- or person-specific? Where do you want to live for two to six months out of the year?

ONE OF THE THINGS THAT I OFTEN SEE ENTREPRENEURS DO is create a "second corporate job" for themselves. They build their business in a way in which everything relies on them. They justify it by saying, "Well, I am working for myself, so it is OK." Instead of working forty-plus hours a week, they are now working fifty to eighty hours a week.

> "Entrepreneurs are the only people who will work eighty hours a week to avoid working forty hours a week."
>
> —LORI GREINER

They say, "It does not feel like work because it is my passion." I used to say that too, as I built and supported a business with team members in five different time zones. My days just got longer and longer trying to support the different markets.

In the beginning when you are really grinding, you may have to do this. However, the long-term plan should require you to off-load your work to other people or automate it. This way, you can enjoy life and follow your dreams. If you design your plan right from the very start to function that way, you will know what you can outsource and will build things differently. Ultimately, you want to have the efforts of two to one hundred people who can work 70 percent to 80 percent as well as you. With this as the goal, you can build, scale, and design your processes to allow you to grow your business.

MAKE YOUR BUSINESS SYSTEM-DEPENDENT AND NOT YOU-DEPENDENT

If the goal for you is to be able to travel more, spend more time with family, etc., then it is important to build a business that is system-dependent. I have worked with people who want to be bicoastal or travel internationally. If that is the goal, it requires putting policies and procedures in place that automate as much of your business as possible, right from the very start.

Technology has made the world flat again. What do I mean by this? Between cell phones and technology (webinar systems, Messenger, etc.) you can work from anywhere in the world and still communicate, function, and run your business. If this is your ultimate goal, you need to plan and build your business that way. You can have the freedom to travel and do what you want, when you want.

This also helps with outsourcing work, from website design to virtual assistants to call centers. One thing to consider is what work/support can be outsourced in the future. This is something you need to keep in mind.

Building a System for Your Business

One exercise I have found helpful when laying out a plan for a business is to build it with the end in mind. This way, you can work backward to create what you need in a timely fashion. I usually take the approach of "let's look five to seven years ahead."

What is your five-year vision for your business?

- How much gross revenue are you generating monthly?

- How much net revenue (after all expenses) do you want monthly?

- How many clients do you have?

- Are you paying yourself a salary?

- How many hours a week are you active in the business?

- How many employees or contractors are working for your business?

- Have you hired a head of operations to run the business?

- What is a skill you will learn or master?

- What will you do for fun?

- What will you do for family or friends?

- Where will you travel to as a reward/work trip?

Now break that down further to your three-year goal, your one-year goal, and your six-month goal by asking the same questions. By working backward, you will actually know what you need to achieve to reach your goal(s). It is important to have fun along your journey and to share this joy with others. Too many people just set goals without fun achievements along the way. In the end, you cannot take it with you, but you can create a lifetime of memories along the way for you, your family, and friends.

Who Do You Need on Your Team?

Most people procrastinate on things they feel they are not good at. They prefer to do things they feel they are good at. Therefore, you should keep doing the things that you like to do and outsource the items or functions you do not like to do.

What is it that you enjoy most about what you do?

- Do you enjoy the sales?

- Do you enjoy creating the strategy?

- Do you enjoy training people or speaking in public?

- Do you enjoy creating the content?

- Do you enjoy building the business and planning?

What do you least enjoy about the business?

- Do you least enjoy the sales?

- Do you least enjoy creating the strategy?

- Do you least enjoy training people or speaking in public?

- Do you least enjoy creating the content?

- Do you least enjoy building the business and planning?

What Skills Do You Need to Hire For?

The things you enjoy the least are the things you should outsource or hire someone else to do. You can find people on Fiverr, Task Rabbit, Upwork, etc. You can do this for some of the more basic tasks. Sometimes your person will grow with you; other times, you need to step up to the next level of outsourcing.

If it is a more important or confidential task, you can go to an outsourcing service. There are companies that will handle your bookkeeping, HR, benefits, etc. You can also hire a virtual assistant. When you are ready to take the function in-house, you can look at hiring someone as a contractor or as a full-time employee. There are additional costs to consider when you hire someone full time, like payroll taxes, benefits, etc.

What Technology Can You Leverage to Support Your Business?

Is there some technology you can leverage to help grow your business? In today's world, there are so many options for you to consider. There are text messaging systems, social media management systems, email systems, sales funnel systems, and customer relationship systems (CRMs), etc. Which way is the best way for you to communicate with your ideal customer?

Based on your ideal customer's age, communication will require different social media platforms. People who are older tend to use Facebook. Younger people use Instagram or Snapchat more. The differences do not stop with social media. This goes for texting, phone calls, email, etc.

Be the CVO for Your Business

I agree with Simon Sinek that the most important thing to do is set the vision for your business. As the owner of the business, it is your job to set the vision for your team and not get sucked into the day-to-day activities. You are the chief visionary officer (CVO) instead of the CEO. The CVO has to set the vision for the company and be able to see far out in the future. It is he/she who determines what will be best for the company. That is why many chief operating officers or chief financial officers do not make good CEOs or CVOs. They are used to dealing with the day-to-day activity instead of looking to the future and seeing the vision. I use the "chicken versus eagle" analogy to describe this situation.

Chickens tend to stay close to the ground and flock together. These are the "workers" in your business. They tend to hang out in groups and work on the daily tasks at hand.

Eagles tend to soar high above the ground alone or in a small group. Eagles have great eyesight and can see storm clouds and prey far off in the distance. CVOs need to be eagles who can guide their company towards success and avoid the storms ahead. They also have to be able to see, swoop down, and take advantage of opportunities before other people see them.

In the beginning, you will need to pitch in on the day-to-day tasks. However, it is important for you to look forward and see the problems and the opportunities ahead. Setting the path for your business and leading from the front sets the tone for your business. As you are building your business, ask yourself, *Am I being a chicken or an eagle?*

I use a real-life training about snorkeling with a turtle and a spotted eagle stingray to show how people often get too focused on the day-to-day activities of their business and do not see the bigger opportunities in the distance. I was snorkeling off the beach in Maui by myself. As I turned back to the beach, there was a big turtle swimming towards me. Some other tourist swam over to see the turtle, but it kept swimming right at me as if to say, "You are in my way and you better move."

As I was filming the encounter with my GoPro, I saw a very faint flash of white in the distance behind the turtle. I almost missed it. I swam over to see what it was, and as I got closer, it turned out to be a spotted eagle stingray. I was able to follow the ray and free dive with it for a few minutes. By the time the tourists saw the stingray, it was already heading back out to sea—they missed it. They had been too distracted by the turtle to see what was happening farther away. To see the video, log in to thelaunchbuttonbook.com and click the "Turtle and Ray" button.

As the CVO, it is your responsibility to see the opportunities in the distance before they pass your business by. You cannot do that if you are focused only on the short-term problems. Make sure you take some time each week to soar like an eagle above your business.

Keep a Narrow Focus of Your Business

One of the problems startups and businesses have is bringing on new products and spreading themselves too wide. This often becomes confusing for employees and customers, and a confused customer does not buy. It is better to stay narrow-focused and build a deep customer base than to have a lot of products and a shallow customer base. You probably have heard, "the riches are in the niches."

Another problem is the continuously changing terms or compensation. If you change them too many times, you will confuse your employees/contractors, and they will become frustrated and turned off. You may think a minor change like going from calling it a "compensation plan" to an "earnings plan" is not a big deal. If you only make this one change, it will take your company's employees/contractors three to six *months* to adopt the new terminology. If you pile on three to six more terminology changes like this, your salesforce might become confused. They may no longer sound professional when they are talking to customers, because they keep correcting themselves or getting corrected. A confused employee or contractor does not want or know how to sell your product/services effectively anymore. This confuses the customer even more. I have watched a company's annual revenue drop almost 50 percent because they continuously changed internal terms in one year.

You want your sales force to be "sharp as a tack." If they are confused, they will not be. Some people will buy your product or service just based on your salesperson's enthusiasm. This is why you want to minimize or keep these changes to three or less a year.

It is important as the CVO to be looking ahead for opportunities and potential pitfalls.

Remember:

1. A confused employee or independent contractor *cannot* effectively sell your product or service.

2. A confused customer or client will *not* buy your product or service.

Saying No to More Things

Inherently, saying yes is not bad, but again, it must be done with discipline. Make sure it is in line with your goals. As you commit to more business events, this can take time, energy, and effort away from building your business. Therefore, I give you permission to say no to more things. Make sure you only say yes to things in line with your goals and vision. That is why it is important to keep them in front of you.

"It's only by saying 'no' that you can concentrate on the things that are really important."

—STEVE JOBS

Over the past fifteen-plus years, I have trained a number of people who have reached high levels of success in their businesses and in real estate investing. Once they do, they are often asked to go out and speak at company events or to other leaders. This is a wonderful honor and a great accomplishment. However, I have seen many people get distracted by these honors, and the next year, their income tanks or drops in half. They feel they must travel and speak at all of the events they are asked to train at. They do not consider what goes into preparing for a presentation or training. Here are a few examples:

- The travel time required to and from the event plus recovery time

- Creating and preparing for the training

- Making sure you have coverage in your business and at home

- Potential time zone and sleeping pattern changes

It takes a lot more planning, energy, and effort than most people realize. This causes people to lose focus on their business, goals, and dreams. That is why you need to plan some fun and family time.

Be selective on where and when you travel for work. The advice I give the people that I have trained is to ask yourself these questions before you agree to speak at an event or training:

1. Will you help build your business and/or expand your team by traveling to this training?

2. Is this a place where you want to take a vacation to?

3. Is there a benefit for growing your business that is greater than the value of your time away from the business?

4. Are you doing this to get seen or for your ego?

If you are struggling with how to answer the last one, I will make it easy for you. If you did not say yes to any of the first three questions, you should not go to speak and/or train at that event, because you are only doing it for your ego. This is where you need to be honest with yourself and determine if your ego is wasting your time.

PRO TIP:
Do Not Be Fuzzy!

One advanced tip as you continue to grow your business is you will need to be very clear with your communication and improve your communication skills. We all think we are great communicators, but we are not. Most people are what I call "fuzzy communicators." They say things that do not answer the question or do not really mean anything.

A couple of years ago, I was having a conversation with one of my millionaire friends, and he stopped me and said, "I have no f&@#ing idea what you just said, and your statement had nothing to do with the question I asked you. Stop wasting my f&@#ing time." Since that week, I have worked hard to clean up my communication process. I have worked hard to improve my team's communication skills, too.

I call it being "fuzzy," which is much nicer than the way he said it to me. My team knows to "Fear the Fuzzy." It has gotten me to really listen to the words people use. People tell you exactly what they want and need if you just listen to their words. *Do not* interrupt their thoughts. Most people have caught themselves thinking or saying, "I think the person meant..." or "They said...but I believe they meant..." Stop thinking and simply ask for clarity.

High-net-worth individuals do not like to waste time. To connect with them, you need to be very clear with your communication. There is a lot more that we can go into, but I will save that for another book. Start listening more, and you will cut down the miscommunication in your business today, which will save you time, energy, and effort. To learn more about "Fear the Fuzzy" training, go to hughzaretsky.com.

CREATING THE LIFESTYLE YOU DESERVE

Now that you have a plan for your business and an idea about the technology that will help you realize your business vision, you can start creating the lifestyle you deserve. The questions is: What is it? Where do you want to live? Do you want to live in more than one location?

Traveling Around the World

Part of the reason to build a business that is systems-dependent is so you can actually enjoy life now, instead of waiting until you retire. As mentioned above, living internationally, bicoastally, or as a snowbird may reduce your tax burdens and save you money. Do you want to be a snowbird, bicoastal, or live internationally for two to six months of the year?

International travel used to be reserved for the rich, but more and more people are doing it. It does not take much to run your business from anywhere in the world. All you need is good Wi-Fi access and cellular service. I have run my business from major cities like New York City, Chicago, Los Angeles, and fun places like the Las Vegas strip, the beaches in Maui, Panama, an RV outside of Joshua Tree, and even from a small village on the island of Lefkada in Greece.

I will ask you again: if money was not an option, where would you love to run your business from?

I do not suggest you buy a place where you want to live part time without testing it first. You should ease into it. The cheapest way to do that is to take a two- to four-week trip to the area. You can think of that first trip as "recon" to see if you like it, and if you can work from there. You need to get to know the locals and the lay of the land. By being there for a few weeks, you can get a good feel for the area before committing to or buying a place. While there you can make connections with real estate agents, property managers, cleaners, and other foreigners living in that area.

> **Note:** Remember the Augusta Rule? Where you can rent out a residence for fourteen days and not pay tax on the profits? You might be able to use this to rent out your home and pay for your travel.

This trip will be a test of your systems and your ability to drive your business from a distance. Most likely, you will not be at a place in your business where you can live for two weeks and not communicate with anyone. Things to consider before you travel:

- **Do you need an international phone or data plan to communicate, or can you just use Wi-Fi?**
  Between text messaging, Facebook Messenger,

WhatsApp, and other apps that can run on Wi-Fi, do you need more ways to communicate?

- **What hours will you be available to work your business or communicate with your team?** It is important to communicate with your team before you leave for your trip. Consider adjusting your work hours or lifestyle to deal with time zone changes, so you can stay in communication with your team. Let me give you two examples:

  * **Lefkada, Greece—five hours ahead of East Coast time (EST):** I was invited on a trip to stay at three villas complete with infinity pools just outside of a little town on Lefkada, a small island in Greece. Lefkada is five hours ahead of East Coast time. This meant adjusting my work schedule to be available from 2:00–7:00 p.m. Lefkada time (9:00 a.m.–2:00 p.m. EST). Any fun activities like boating, snorkeling, pirate ships, parties, etc. would either occur in the morning or after 7:00 p.m.

  * **Maui, Hawaii—five or six hours behind East Coast time:** Each February, I travel to Hawaii and often go to Maui for a couple of weeks. Maui is five hours behind EST, so I make sure I am available from 8:00 a.m.–1:00 p.m. HST (1:00–5:00 p.m. EST). Hawaii does not adjust for daylight saving time. This means when the rest of the US springs forward an hour, Hawaii does not change, which creates a six-hour time gap.

Before I leave for my trips to different time zones, I plan out and let my team know which hours I will be available to coordinate with them to have meetings, conference calls, webinars, etc. This way, everyone can be prepared and adjust their schedules accordingly. This gives my team specific time blocks for them to schedule meetings without having to contact me in advance. This also allows me time to have fun. This consideration allows my business and team to continue to grow with confidence when I am traveling.

After your trip, it is important to do an evaluation of how your team performed and where there were holes in your business. You need to fix and close those holes.

THE EVALUATION

EXTERNAL: THE LOCATION	INTERNAL: YOUR BUSINESS
Did you like the area and have fun?	Were your staff or systems able to run the majority of the business without you?
Could you see yourself working from the area?	Have you established clear escalation plans for problems in your business?
Did it have the amenities that you needed to run your business?	Does your staff know where these procedures are and have access to them?
Were you able to communicate with your team clearly?	Do they know what issues they should contact you for and what issues they have the power to answer for themselves?

The next step is to schedule your second trip to that area, but this time, plan to spend one or two months. Now that you know the lay of the land and have established some connections, you can typically find a better deal on a place to stay in the area that you want to eventually live in. You also know the prime season for the market, the low season, and the shoulder or gap season. Most of the time, you can get a great deal during the low season and shoulder season as there are more properties available. Owners are also more willing to discount the price of the rent or short-term rental rate if you book for a longer stay like thirty days or more.

This trip will be more important to test your business habits, your schedule maintenance, and your team's performance as you work remotely. You need to make sure you can continue to build your business while working remotely from your new location. Not all travel requires this much planning, but you want your team prepared for your travel schedule and to be able to function smoothly. Remember, confused people do not build or sell.

If your second trip is going well and you are enjoying your time, make some time to meet with real estate agents, property managers, and attorneys. Or, at least get some referrals while you are in the area. It is always better to meet face to face while you are in the area with these contacts even if it is just for coffee. This way, you are not just a voice over the phone.

After this trip, you need to do the same evaluation you did after your first trip. What went well? And what did not? Did your team know how to escalate issues and handle any emergencies? What policies and procedures do you need to update?

After your second trip, you should know if you just want to keep visiting the area or stay longer. If you do want to stay longer, then you may want to make an investment in a second home, a vacation rental, or investment property. This gives you the freedom to travel when you want and then rent out the property to generate income. At this point, you should have a good idea of the area or areas that you want to stay in and have built some local connections with real estate agents, management companies, and/or property owners. This will make it easier to acquire a property.

If not, do your homework and research the market before you head over for your third trip. You might be able to acquire something in your target area before your trip or at least be able to line up showings and potential deals. That way, you can look at the properties in person on your trip. Remember, this can become another source of income if you run your numbers and understand the market. It does not matter if you buy a property or rent and re-rent. You want to make sure that you have the ability to rent the place while you are not using it. This way, you can at least cover your expenses and/or make a profit. This just adds another revenue stream to your income.

Your third trip to the area should be the final test for your business systems and scheduling. You may want to increase the length of your time away from your team to a few weeks to six months. You should be able to maintain your lifestyle, grow your business, and make things happen for you and your family. You now have work freedom. Congratulations on achieving your goal!

I go to Hawaii every February because it is the worst time of the year to be in New York City, in my opinion. February is usually cold, gray, and snowy. This is why my business requires a training for my team members in Hawaii in February. I usually do multiple trainings and spread them out. Sometimes they are on Maui and sometimes on multiple islands. It depends on my team as well as my opportunities while I am there.

I created my schedule so that working from Hawaii does not really impact my business. I still run my daily and weekly conference calls and trainings, meetings, etc. The big difference is that instead of dealing with the cold (ten to thirty-two degrees Fahrenheit), gray skies, snow, and wind of NYC, I can walk down to the beach and snorkel or dive in the sixty-eight- to eighty-five-degree weather of Hawaii. Something about being in the water or on the water allows me to be more present in what I am doing. Having my afternoons free to meditate, snorkel, scuba, run, work out, and so on also helps. My time in Hawaii allows me to slow down and be more creative for my business, and it keeps me invigorated to drive my business when I return to NYC. All of this allows me to be a more effective leader.

SHORT-TERM OR LONG-TERM RENTAL

The question is: do you acquire a short-term or a long-term rental property? If you want to be able to use your place often, then I would suggest going the shared economy route and using short-term rentals. There are a couple different ways that you can manage your properties. The most common options are:

- Do it yourself

- Cohost

- Full service

Do It Yourself

If you have the time to do it yourself, then it will require additional time to manage your listing, guest communication, pricing, and maintenance of the unit. How much time do you have to dedicate to doing this?

- Hire two cleaners for your units

- Hire a maintenance person

- Quickly respond to guest inquires 24/7

- Maintain your pricing during the busy and slow seasons

- Prioritize through calendar management

- Maintain post-guest communication

- Keep up with Airbnb reservations

Hire a Cohosting Service

They will handle all of the online communication with guests, pricing, calendar, Airbnb reservations, etc. The only thing you will have to handle is the cleaners and maintaining the unit. This is something you most likely want to do so you can know if there are any issues with your unit.

Full-Service Hosting

They handle everything for you, including scheduling the cleaners and minor maintenance of the unit.

> **Note:** Which option do you prefer? If you are going to hire someone, then I suggest interviewing two to three different companies to determine which one best fits your needs. It does not matter if you buy the property or lease and re-lease it. You will still need to establish some sort of management for the property while you are not there. This way it can generate revenue and provide you with additional income. Go to CoHostingPro.com to get more information on cohosting and full-service options.

Remember:

1. A confused employee or independent contractor cannot effectively sell your product or service.

2. A confused customer or client will *not* buy your product or service.

It may take you more than one positive-cash-flowing property before you can replace your income or press the launch button from your job. You can either repeat the steps in this chapter for a second property or see the bonus section on how to scale and go full nomad!

EXERCISE:
Assets You Can Leverage
and Tax-Reduction Strategies

Do you want your answers in a digital format? If so, go to thelaunchbuttonbook.com and log in to create your own The Launch Button Blueprint for Success PDF!

- Create your five-year vision for your business. Use the questions earlier in the chapter to create your plan:

    * Who do you need on your team?

    * What skills do you need to hire for?

    * What technology can you leverage to support your business?

- What is the vision for your business?

- What did you learn from your first test evaluation?

STAYING IN ORBIT

STAGE 2

13

Implement the Lifestyle of Your Dreams: Press the Launch Button from Your Job!

Eject from Your Job!

The big day is here! Knowing when to press the Launch Button and "Fire Your Boss." This is when it costs you more money to go to work than to stay home.

ARE YOU READY TO TEAR THE BAND-AID OFF AND FIRE YOUR boss?

Throughout this journey, you have started to see and taste the benefits of launching your business and adding cash flow to your life. It is now time for Stage 2, while continuing to stay in orbit. Your income from your business should now be almost equal to your take-home pay or your salary. You should be making as much money part time as you are full time. Before you fire your boss, let's review one last checklist to make sure you have everything in place that you may need or want.

Let's start with your safety nets. Have you set these up and funded the ones that you want?

- **Is your "Oh Crap Account" fully funded with at least six months of expenses?** This will give you and/or your spouse a significant amount of peace, knowing there is a safety net so you will not lose your house.

- **Is your overfunded whole life insurance properly set up for you?** You want this plan to be overfunded in very conservative investments to give you a balance between your business and real estate deals. These policies also give you the ability to fund your business or real estate deals and borrow from your own policy. It provides an additional safety net for you and provides a legacy for your family.

- **Do you have the financing you want in place?** Do you have all the loans, lines of credit, and credit cards you feel you will need to fund your business and lifestyle? This is the one thing that most people tend to forget. Once you no longer have a traditional W-2 job, your access to funding becomes harder to get during the first two years of your business. Therefore, you want to make sure you have acquired your loans, lines of credit, and credit cards before you fire your boss. You may want to ask for increases on all your current lines before you fire your boss, as well. That way you are maximizing all your opportunities.

Let's get into protection.

- **Is your health insurance set up?** Make sure you have a plan for this. If you need an international plan, there are certain additional things to consider. Telemedicine has come a long way over the years.

- **Have you established your self-directed retirement accounts (SDRA)?** You want these established before you fire your boss so you can roll over your current accounts at your job to your NEW SDRA. This rollover process can take anywhere from two to eight weeks. Your old 401(k) company may attempt to frighten or scare you and make it hard to make this transition. I have seen some people really get messed up by leaving their old retirement accounts at their old jobs and then not be able to get their money moved to their new accounts.

> * You should have already met with your CPA or tax professionals to have retirement plans in place for your new business(es). For me, it was to set up a genuine self-directed Roth 401(k) plan. This allowed me to roll the 401(k) plan from my "old job" into the traditional side and then to establish my new Roth for my personal matching.

- **Do you have a will and testament?** Everyone needs a will and testament to ensure you pass on your business and properties to your family or whoever you want them to go to. You may have assets that no one else knows you have as you are growing your business. Make sure all of your assets are listed in your will and testament. Most states require this to be notarized. Make sure it is updated, as circumstances will change when you leave your job and launch your new business.

IS YOUR BUSINESS AND PASSIVE INCOME ENOUGH TO COVER YOUR BILLS AND SUPPORT YOUR LIFESTYLE?

This is going to be your "new" salary. You want this amount to at least replace your current job's income. That way, you can keep enjoying the lifestyle you deserve. There are only a few reasons to leave your job before you have replaced your income. Some examples are a major problem with your boss, change in economy, change in family, or your health. If the stress of your job is having a significant negative effect on the rest of your life, then push the launch button sooner.

I have found that when people start building a side hustle, they become less affected by the stress at their job. When you already know that you have additional income, you no longer get stressed out as much.

Note: This makes you happier and able to focus on the things that you enjoy, like your side hustle.

Do You Have a Succession Plan for Your New Business?

As the CVO of your new business, you may need to investigate another type of insurance called "key man" insurance.

Key Man Insurance

If, God forbid, something were to happen to you, would your family or contractors know where everything is or what needs to happen to keep your business going? Most of the time that answer is no. That is why you want to look into key man insurance—a life insurance policy that companies purchase on the life of an owner, a top executive, or another individual considered critical to the business. This type of life insurance is also known as key man (or keyman) insurance, key woman insurance, and business life insurance. Most people want their business to stay in orbit and provide a legacy for their family.

To retire into the lap of luxury, it is important that you groom someone to eventually take over your role in the company. This could be in two years or ten years, depending on what you want to do and how you want to do it. This is another thing for you to think about as you prepare to press the launch button.

Leaving your corporate job will create a hole in your previous company. They may hire someone or have a succession plan for your role. You will need to do the same thing when you eventually step back from running your own business.

How Are You Going to Give Notice?

If you have verified that you have everything in place, you can shift your focus to how you are going to press the launch button and fire your boss. I want you to consider how people in similar positions were exited from your company. This is important because it is most likely how you will be treated. Some companies allow you to stay on the job all the way through to the end of your notice time. In other companies, people are told to pack their stuff and leave the same day that they give notice. It just depends on the company and your role there. Most companies have standard operating policies and procedures for how they handle employees who have given notice. Do not expect special treatment. What has your company done to people in similar positions or in your department?

If there is even a slight chance that you will be ushered out the door the same day you give notice, here are a few things you should do in advance of giving notice:

1. **Clear your personal files from your computer or the office cloud system:** You may want to make a copy of your personal files onto a flash drive, Google Drive, Dropbox, etc. If you email them to yourself, then remember to go into your sent folder and delete them from there, as well.

2. **Clear any personal messages from your work email system:** You will want to clear out any personal messages, work email, and personal email addresses.

3. **Slowly take home any "knickknacks" or personal things you want from your cubicle or office:** You want to do this slowly so it does not bring attention to the fact that you may be leaving. This way, when you do give notice and they offer to box up your belongings and ship them to you, you will already have the most valuable assets at home. Sometimes, things get lost or broken in shipping. This will protect your items of value.

4. **Contact information:** Depending on your role, there may be contacts at work, your customers, vendors, etc. or people that you definitely want to stay in touch with. Make sure you have their cell phone numbers and personal email addresses before you give notice. You may have a second list of the "maybes." So make sure you get as many "maybes" contact information as you can before you give notice too.

5. **Letters of reference:** If you want any letters of reference, testimonials, etc. from coworkers, you should ask and get a copy of them before you give notice.

6. **Bonuses of any kind:** If you receive a yearly or a performance bonus, then this is also a consideration before you give notice. If you will get paid your bonus soon, then you may want to wait until you receive that bonus. If it is four to six months or more away, then you may not care.

7. **Maintaining relationships:** We all know relationships are tricky and you do not want to burn them. That is why it is important to consider which relationships you want to maintain. I heard a great quote from Jesse Itzler: "Be nice to everyone in your twenties and thirties because you never know who is going to rise to power in their forties." That is why it is very important to maintain your relationships and to stay in touch with people. You never know who can help you connect with someone in the future. This is also why it is important that you are careful to not burn too many relationships when you fire your boss.

Now, the last thing to consider is *when* you will give notice. How will that affect your relationships with your boss, your boss's boss, your team, and so on? If you are leaving to pursue your dream, they all should be happy for you as long as you gave notice the right way. Consider the following questions before you give notice:

- How many weeks' notice (two to four) will you give? In most jobs, two weeks is the minimum.

- How will they respond?

- Will they be happy for you?

- Will they be upset?

You still want to give the proper amount of notice, even if you will be escorted out the door that day. Your boss will appreciate it, and it is the right thing to do. It is up to the company to honor it. If they walk you out the door the same day, most will still give you two additional weeks of pay, and you get to start building the life you deserve immediately.

EXERCISE:
The Big Day: How Are You Going to Do It?

If you want your answers in a digital PDF, then log into thelaunchbuttonbook.com to create your own The Launch Button Blueprint for Success PDF!

- Is your Oh Crap Account fully funded with six months of expenses?

- Is your overfunded whole life insurance properly set up for you?

- Do you have the financing you want in place?

- Is your health insurance set up?

- Have you established your self-directed retirement accounts (SDRAs)?

- Do you have a will and testament?

- Do you have everything you want from your office?

- How are you going to give notice?

14

Go Big or Go Back to the 50x40x40

Go Big or Go Back to Your Job!

How big do you want to build your business, or are you happy with your income and now want to dedicate your time to a charity or a cause?

YOU ARE READY TO "GO BIG OR GO BACK TO YOUR 50x40x40!" If you have done all of the exercises, then you are ready to stay in orbit! It is time to create FOMO (fear of missing out).

LETTING THE WORLD KNOW YOU FIRED YOUR BOSS AND CREATE FOMO

You should feel comfortable building and growing your business. It is time to tell the world. Leverage that to market your brand, business, products, etc. You want to create FOMO for all of your colleagues, family, friends, etc. Be prepared to capitalize on this opportunity and the momentum it will create.

When you announce you have pressed the launch button and walked away from your job, there will be a lot of questions. The best way to keep the momentum going is to allow people to see and understand what you have built. You might even create an event for them to attend. This will save you time, and at least one person will want to buy your product/services and/or join your team. This will start the herd mentality, and some of your other friends or peers will join as well.

How Are You Going to Celebrate?

In planning the Big Day—your last day on the job—you need to reward yourself for taking action, cutting the umbilical cord, and freeing yourself from the matrix of the 50x40x40 world. What is your immediate reward going to be for reaching your goal? I have known some people who have planned a trip around the world, thrown a party, hired a limo to pick them up from work, etc.

What are you going to do for your family? Who do you want to celebrate with you? If you do not take them on a trip, are you going to give them something for dealing with your craziness over the past few months or years? They deserve a reward for putting up with you while you were working your nine-to-five and your side hustle. What are you going to get or do for them?

Earlier, we talked about momentum and how important that is for your business. If you are entering the busy time of the year, you may schedule your big celebration for a slower time of the year. You need to have a big trip, event, or something to mark this special occasion in your life. The goal is to only have to fire your boss once. Sometimes it may happen that you have to do it again. And that is OK!

A few things to remember:

- **Be the chief visionary officer:** It is your role to decide the future of your business, family, etc. and to build the vision that you want your life to be or the life that you deserve. Life is going to test you now that you are changing your routine. Remember the chicken vs. the eagle? Do not get distracted by life and lose focus on your long-term goals. As the CVO, it is important to keep the future vision in focus and available to your team as well.

- **You need to treat your business like a business:** This means implementing all of the things that we talked about in this book and keeping your self-discipline, your goals, and your vision for your business in front of you. Treat your business like a business, and it will pay you like a business. Treat it like a hobby, and it will cost you like a hobby. Once you fire your boss, you will need to go even harder and ride the momentum and excitement that you have just created.

- **Protect your work schedule:** One of the hardest things for some entrepreneurs is sticking to a schedule once they fire their boss and are no longer working the 50x40x40. They want to rebel because they just left their corporate job and do not want to be stuck to a schedule. I talked about the reassociations and how to build your new habits to support your business and get into new patterns or routines. You must create nonnegotiable work time and block it out on your schedule. Otherwise, life and the universe will take control of your schedule.

- **Play the infinity game:** Make sure you are making decisions that will benefit your business, your family, and your legacy for future generations.

No matter how much you plan and prepare for all kinds of different scenarios, life will always throw you a curveball to test your desired goal or dream. You will need to call a few audibles along that way. *Audibles* is a football term for adjusting on the fly or quickly. It is important that you have a clear vision of where you want to go so you can call the right audibles. These challenges will continue to happen in your business, and you will need to adjust along the way.

EXERCISE:
Go Big or Go Back to 50x40x40

If you want your answers in a digital PDF, then log into thelaunchbuttonbook.com to create your own The Launch Button Blueprint for Success PDF!

- **What do you consider to be your "go big" goal?**

- **Are you planning your FOMO announcement and giving notice on that day?**

- **Are you playing the infinity game and planning to leave your business to future generations?**

- **Have you created your nonnegotiable work time?**

- **Have you created your boundaries on your schedule?**

Conclusion

CONGRATULATIONS ON READING THIS BOOK AND CREATING A blueprint plan that will launch your business into outer space! You should be excited to create the life you deserve. Remember, you have built an action plan and daily habits that will help you reach success faster. If you break one of your habits one day, that is OK; just start a new streak the very next day. Do not allow one day to grow into two or three days. You should also be prepared for the entrepreneur roller coaster and how to stay even-keeled through the process.

As you go through your entrepreneur journey, you will most likely have to come back and review certain parts of this book. Give yourself permission to make some audibles. Do not hesitate to come back to read a certain section for a second, third, or more times. Remember, you are playing the long game of life or the infinity game, and most of the time, you will not see results right away. Keep your vision in front of you. If you are persistent, you will get what you deserve. If you are consistent, then you will achieve the lifestyle, the business, and the income that you deserve. Consistent, daily action will have you transforming your business into the business of your dreams. Just like working out, you may not see results the next day, but you will over time. This is the same with your business. Keep working on your vision every day to make it better.

Whenever you get stuck, it is important to remember your hidden deep "why" that caused you to start this journey. Allowing yourself to feel the emotions of not fulfilling your why should motivate you to get back on track.

Remember, it could be as simple as one more phone call, connection, ad, or conversation that will take your business to the next level. Taking one more step past your "quitting mind" or fear is where you will find success. Once your mind understands that you will not quit, that is when it flips and accepts your "new normal." Your brain says, "OK, let's make this goal or dream happen."

I cannot tell you how many stories I have heard like this of someone about ready to quit who finally fought through their thoughts, feelings, etc., and broke through to reach their goal. Just remember that you can do it, because you want to create the life you deserve.

Stay plugged into the eFramily Facebook group, and I look forward to helping you along your journey to success. If you want support from a group of entrepreneurs, then you can join us at eFramily.com. You will get ongoing support from this platform from webinars and a community of entrepreneurs, as well as additional training and content.

Please let me know if there is anything I can do to help you create the life that you deserve.

You can always quit. It is the easiest thing you can do. So, why quit now? Just take one more action towards building the life you deserve.

Bonus: Get your free "nomad" bonus section by logging into **thelaunchbuttonbook.com** and click the "Nomad Bonus" button.

Acknowledgments

FOURTEEN YEARS AGO, I KNEW I HAD TO WRITE THIS BOOK. I finally gave myself permission to do it. I want to acknowledge and thank the many people who helped me along the way.

My parents, Dayle and Irwin, for always setting a good example for their children. My brother, Ari, and my sister, Missy, for always supporting me and each other, even when we did not always agree. I could not ask for better siblings. My entire extended family: Myles, Ava, Harper, Glen, Jacs, John, Andi, Scott, and all of my cousins, aunts, and uncles. My journey was not a straight path, but you all were always there for me. Thank you!

I want to thank all of my Binghamton University friends for the past twenty-plus years of their friendship. You were there for me in the good and bad times. The shenanigans will always remain a secret. A few of you made it into the book but understand all of your friendships mean a lot to me. My friends from Getty Images will always share the bond of 9/11. Special thanks to all of my softball and soccer friends over the years in NYC. I appreciate all of your support and the "just one mores!"

Thank you to Edna Bautista and Tony for seeing a speaker/trainer inside of a corporate IT executive. Thanks to Joe G, Mike, Ted, and Jen for teaching me how to present, showing me the ropes of the business, and being great friends. Thanks to Jen, Rob, Angela, and Troy for being great trainers, friends, and partners on the road. Thanks to Chris Albin for introducing me to Bob Snyder and his terrific company. Thanks, Nanci and Scott R, and Bob T for trusting me with your Chicago community for years. A special thanks to the rest of my former FAB and PAC members who helped shape a great organization and a community.

A special thanks to my BEST team and eFramily Ohana members for being with me for the last ten-plus years. To my students all around the world, thank you for trusting me and the process. You have stayed with me as entrepreneurs and real estate investors through the years. You have allowed me to refine my trainings and theories as I created version 2.0. I have included some of you and those trainings in this book. There are also some new ones that you have never heard of before. I appreciated your trust and support over the years, and I truly appreciate each and every one of you. You know who you are.

Thank you to Cassie, my catch-all person. She has helped me get organized and kept me on task to complete this book. Special thanks to all of my private team of editors: Pat M, Cassie, Mom and Dad, Aunt Viv, and Jill L. You helped transform my manuscript while maintaining my voice and personality in this book. Thank you, Garret Gunderson for giving me the final push to write this book and connecting me with Tucker Max and Scribe Media. I have to thank Scribe Media for their process and professional editing of this book. Thanks, Hal, Emily, John, Tucker, Kayla, Lisa C., and many more. It was a pleasure working with everyone on your team.

Thank you to Daniel Grillone for your wonderful sketches that helped bring this book to life.

As they say, "Teamwork makes the dream work" and this book would not be possible without all of you.

Thank you,

Hugh

Resources

"The 'Uber Effect' Is Crushing Taxi Medallion Prices and Spilling Over into Public Markets." CBInsights. October 1, 2015. https://www.cbinsights.com/research/public-stock-driven-uber/.

Avery, Daniel. 2019. "A Record Number of Americans Are Traveling Abroad." *Newsweek*, March 28, 2019. https://www.newsweek.com/record-number-americans-traveling-abroad-1377787.

Chen, James. 2021. "Income Tax Term Guide: Passive Income." Investopedia. February 12, 2021. https://www.investopedia.com/terms/p/passiveincome.asp.

Cohan, William D. 2012. "What's Really Going on With Mitt Romney's $102 Million IRA." *The Atlantic*, September 10, 2012. https://www.theatlantic.com/politics/archive/2012/09/whats-really-going-on-with-mitt-romneys-102-million-ira/261500/.

eFramily Ohana. https://www.eframily.com/.

Kagan, Julia. 2021. "Income Tax Term Guide: Active Income." Investopedia. March 31, 2021. https://www.investopedia. com/terms/a/activeincome.asp.

Marr, Bernard. 2016. "The Sharing Economy—What It Is, Examples, and How Big Data, Platforms and Algorithms Fuel It." *Forbes*, October 21, 2016. https://www.forbes.com/ sites/bernardmarr/2016/10/21/the-sharing-economy-what-it-is-examples-and-how-big-data-platforms-and-algorithms-fuel/?sh=609182727c5a.

National Small Business Association. 2018. *NSBA 2017 Year-End Economic Report.* Washington, DC: NSBA, 2018. https:// nsba.biz/wp-content/uploads/2018/02/Year-End-Economic-Report-2017.pdf.

Ricciulli, Valeria. 2019. "City Vows to Crack Down on Predatory Taxi Medallion Brokers." *Curbed New York*, July 8, 2019. https://ny.curbed.com/2019/7/8/20686319/nyc-taxi-medallion-owners-brokers-predatory-practices-tlc.

Roser, Max. 2017. "Tourism." OurWorldInData.org. 2017. https:// ourworldindata.org/tourism#citation.

TradersAccounting.com Research. 2021. "$7,000 of Tax-Free Income Every Year." TradersLog.com. 2021. https://www. traderslog.com/taxfree.

Zaretsky, Hugh. 2020. *Steps to Fire Your Boss—5 Week Productivity Journal.* New York: Royal Empire Ventures, Inc.

Zaretsky, Hugh. https://hughzaretsky.com/.

CPSIA information can be obtained
at www.ICGtesting.com
Printed in the USA
LVHW101929211022
731268LV00013B/239/J